D0114452

☆ LEONARD ☆
MARSHALL
THE END OF THE LINE

GV939
.M294
A3
1987

☆LEONARD☆ MARSHALL

THE END OF THE LINE

by Leonard Marshall and Dave Klein

With an Introduction by Bill Parcells

NAL BOOKS

NEW AMERICAN LIBRARY

NEW YORK AND SCARBOROUGH, ONTARIO

Copyright © 1987 by Leonard Marshall and Dave Klein

All rights reserved. For information address New American Library.

Published simultaneously in Canada by The New American Library of Canada Limited.

 NAL BOOKS TRADEMARK REG. U.S. PAT. OFF. AND FOREIGN COUNTRIES
REGISTERED TRADEMARK—MARCA REGISTRADA
HECHO EN CHICAGO, U.S.A.

SIGNET, SIGNET CLASSIC, MENTOR, ONYX, PLUME, MERIDIAN
and NAL BOOKS are published *in the United States* by NAL PENGUIN INC.,
1633 Broadway, New York, New York 10019,
in Canada by The New American Library of Canada Limited,
81 Mack Avenue, Scarborough, Ontario M1L 1M8

Library of Congress Cataloging-in-Publication Data

Marshall, Leonard.
  Leonard Marshall: the end of the line.

  1. Marshall, Leonard.   2. Football players—United
States—Biography.   I. Klein, Dave.   II. Title.
GV939.M294A3   1987   796.332′092′4 [B]   87-18526
ISBN 0-453-00576-4

Designed by Leonard Telesca

First Printing, September, 1987

1   2   3   4   5   6   7   8   9

PRINTED IN THE UNITED STATES OF AMERICA

For Annette, and for my parents
—L.M.

323, and for my late brother, Barry
—D.K.

ACKNOWLEDGMENTS

I would like to give special thanks to God for the courage, strength and spirit He has given me. Also, special thanks to my wife, Annette, and to her mom and dad and family, and to my parents, whose love and guidance has been crucial to my success. And thanks to all my brothers and sisters. Last of all, thanks to my good friend, Dave Klein.

—L.M.

I would like to thank my agent, Dominick Abel, for smoothing out all the rough spots; Dick Shanahan, for "crisis intervention" when the Canon decided I was so unqualified that it wouldn't perform; and Kevin Mulroy, the editor of this book, who was helpful from start to finish.

—D.K.

We would both like to thank several people for making this job reasonably easy. Marvin Brown and Maryann Palumbo, of course, for approving the project. Ken Wirth, Leonard's advisor; Bill Strasser, his attorney; New York Giants' head coach Bill Parcells, for providing us with the favor of an introduction when all around him other writers and athletes were asking for the same consideration; and to the Newark Airport Marriott, for providing us with the peace and quiet of a pleasant oasis in a setting equidistant from our homes.

CONTENTS

☆LEONARD☆
MARSHALL
THE END OF THE LINE

INTRODUCTION

When I drafted Leonard Marshall in the second round of the 1983 draft, I remember feeling extremely lucky and a little surprised to have had the opportunity. We had given Leonard a first-round grade as a defensive lineman from Louisiana State University, and our scouting department is very conservative in making that kind of decision. We decided we had two needs in the early rounds of that draft—a safety to groom for the eventual replacement of a veteran named Beasley Reece, and a defensive end to replace one I had just traded to the Los Angeles Rams, Gary Jeter.

We had zeroed in on Clemson safety Terry Kinard and Leonard Marshall as our top choices for those two positions. When our turn came up, in the tenth position on the first round, both players were still there. We took Kinard, and I figured that we had definitely lost our chance to get Leonard, too, because we weren't scheduled to draft again until the ninth spot in the second round.

In fact, we had kind of settled on another defensive lineman, Mike Charles of Syracuse, as a possible consideration for that second-round selection. There were two or three others, but we thought they'd be gone, like Gabriel Rivera of Texas Tech and Mike Pitts of Alabama.

So you can imagine how surprised and pleased I was that Leonard was still unclaimed when we had our next chance to select. We took him quickly, and when that draft was over, I felt that the New York Giants had actually acquired two first-round-quality draft picks.

Why was Leonard still there in the second round? Frankly, I don't know. He played well in his junior and senior seasons at LSU, had a good work ethic and work habits, wasn't difficult to coach and was very strong and quick. Some people seem to think that defensive ends should be taller: Leonard is only 6–3, and most defensive ends coming out these days are 6–5, 6–6, up around there.

In fact, several people thought we might try to convert Leonard to nose tackle, and although I think he would be a good one, perhaps even outstanding, I didn't have any plans for that. In our defensive system, the tall and rangy defensive ends probably don't make it as easily as those somewhat shorter but intensely strong and solid, especially when they have great strength in their lower body.

We need our defensive ends to play inside, to "two-gap" on many formations, and the tall, thin ones just aren't equipped for that. So in our scheme of things, Leonard was the perfect size for a defensive end. We're fortunate that other teams use different systems, I guess.

Things weren't easy for Leonard at the beginning. He's just a big kid, a big teddy-bear kind of kid, and he came up here all smiles and grins. And overweight. And not in proper physical condition. He didn't have the slightest idea how much work it was going to take to play in the National Football League.

I told the press the night of the draft that they were going to like this one, that we might have to weigh him at one of those truck stops on the New Jersey Turnpike. It was a joke and wasn't meant to be unkind, but it became exaggerated.

Anyway, we put Leonard on a controlled intake of food, and I have to say that he showed me great determination and drive. He was out of condition, no two ways about that. He wasn't that much overweight, although he was ten to fifteen pounds too heavy, but he wasn't in game shape. We got him there eventually, and he worked as hard as he possibly could, as hard as I would have hoped, but it cost him some time, and he didn't play much that entire season.

People thought we had made a mistake drafting him that high, but I think Leonard's hard work and dedication to his job has vindicated all of us. He has been voted to the Pro Bowl the past two years—two of the four seasons that he has been in the NFL—and he is getting better each game. Leonard has great strength and drive, he is a smart player and he works beautifully with Lawrence Taylor, the outside linebacker on his side. With those two, I don't worry that much about the right side of the defense, although people will tell you I worry about defense all the time.

At this point in his career, I would consider Leonard to be one of the best defensive ends in the league. After all, two consecutive years in the Pro Bowl says that, doesn't it? Also, he has the capacity and the capability to get better, to become more of a force, more of a dynamic player.

I count Leonard as one of my friends, too. I am proud to know him, I have been delighted to work with him and I am sure he will be better this season than he was in 1986, our Super Bowl season.

Bill Parcells
Giants' Head Coach
East Rutherford, New Jersey
May 1987

CHAPTER 1

"I guess Carson wasn't used to being turned down by a rookie; he picked up a bowl of my usual meal—cottage cheese—and flung it in my face."

NO PIECE OF CAKE FOR THE FAT KID

When the New York Giants drafted me in 1983, I wasn't sure at first whether I was being acquired as a defensive lineman or the team mascot. Nobody had to remind me that football is a rough sport, but I never expected a newspaper story to knock me on my ass. But there it was, in black and white: "Wait until you see this Marshall kid," Giant coach Bill Parcells was quoted as saying. "We're gonna have to weigh this one at a truck station on the Jersey Turnpike."

Parcells went on to tell the press (and the world) that I was "undisciplined, as a result overweight, and as a result of that, much too slow."

At first I thought, was this some kind of April Fool's joke—four weeks late? Had they drafted me, then changed their mind, and were now planning to dump me at the first opportunity? Why was Parcells saying that I was "slower than erosion"? If this was the Giants' way of getting rookies to be mean and ugly, they were doing a good job on me.

Finally, Parcells was asked, "Why did you draft him then, if he's got a weight problem?"

"Because we think he can play," he said. "Because we think he can be an outstanding defensive lineman, and because if we can keep him in shape, he's going to help us for a long time."

At least he wasn't kidding about keeping me in shape. (Months later I learned that he had instructed defensive line coach Lamar Leachman and strength and condition-ing coach Johnny Parker to "get on him and stay on him" in summer training camp.) Parcells did not need to remind himself to "ride Marshall"—it came naturally. Parcells' coaching philosophy dictates that some athletes need to be stroked, others need to be kicked. As I would soon learn, his decision was that Leonard Marshall needed to be kicked.

After I had showed up at camp and the coaches had let everybody know that I was overweight and out of shape, things got pretty nasty. Lamar had been on me ever since Day One, constantly bugging me with the fat-and-lazy-and-out-of-shape-and-too-damned-rich stuff. It took a long time, but I finally lost control. It was a meeting at training camp and Lamar just kept pouring it on and, I mean, that was it. I really went after him. I remember it was (defen-sive end) George Martin who held me back. He wrapped his arms around me and said something like, "Hey, Leon-ard, you don't want to be doing this. You don't." Now Lamar is one of my best friends and we laugh at that first summer, but I'll tell you this: I think we're both glad I didn't get to him.

The Giants hold summer training camp on the campus of Pace University in Pleasantville, New York, home of *Reader's Digest* and Foley's Tavern, two of its most popu-lar landmarks. It seemed to me that more than a few players joined in my hazing, because in a way that's what it was, and to some degree that's what it comes down to for all rookies.

Harry Carson, the veteran linebacker who has been to the Pro Bowl eight times, is generally in charge of tormenting rookies. The most popular game is to make a rookie stand on his chair after the evening meal in the cafeteria and sing his college song. Early in camp, when Carson decided it was my turn, I refused. Why? Because I didn't think I needed to be doing that shit, because I didn't want to and because I didn't think it was part of what I was. So I told him no, I won't do that.

I guess he wasn't used to being turned down by a rookie; he picked up a bowl of my usual meal—cottage cheese—and flung it in my face. Maybe that's why he got involved in those Gatorade dumpings on coach Parcells. Maybe he has a natural talent for throwing food. Anyway, everything was quiet for a minute, dead silence. Nobody said a thing, rookies or veterans. Harry and I stood there staring at each other, and I know it was a kind of moment of truth for me. I had challenged the system, and a kind of tradition that nobody had messed with before.

I reached a decision, and I think it was a result of all the frustration and tension. I just took off after Carson, and there wasn't much college-boy fooling around in this, no fraternity fun. I wanted to kill him. People held me down, stopped me, and that was a good thing for Harry. That was the final push, and I wasn't going to take any more. I deserved respect. I was prepared to fight for it. Nobody was laughing then, man, it was serious. My intentions were to nail him, and I threatened him, threatened to get even.

Much later I found out that Harry had been put up to the riding of the fat-kid rookie by Parcells. I guess it finally worked. I suddenly realized what they wanted from me, what they expected of me. I found direction and purpose, if only because of the humiliation by my peers. Now

Parcells had to step in. He explained to me that the Giants do not threaten each other, do not carry a grudge, that we are one big family and things that happen, personal things, are supposed to be forgotten and forgiven.

Bill Parcells: "We needed to get Leonard motivated. This wasn't some kind of fun camp we were running for rich kids. This game is really a tough job, a job for grown men. I don't think you can be too well adjusted if you're going to play professional football, but you've got to be able to focus everything, your thoughts and your intensity and your concentration, on the job at hand. If you start to feel sorry for yourself, if you think you can take things easy because you're big and strong and nobody has ever been able to stop you before, then you are about to become a former pro football player. I have never seen a rookie come into this league—no matter how great an athlete—properly prepared to experience what it's like. Oh, sure, some of them show up in the NFL and they become instant stars. Lawrence Taylor, for instance. But they still don't have any idea of what to expect. Guys in college, All-America types, have pretty much decided they're great people, great athletes, can't teach them anything, you know? Then they show up in camp and some thirty-four-year-old guy looks at them, kind of sneers and puts them on the grass with a forearm shiver. It's a whole new world. They've got to learn fast about the pressure and the competition. Guys earn a living doing this. They don't have practice and then go to algebra and then to the soda shop and show each other their letter sweaters. This is real, and for every hotshot rookie who makes the team, some ten-year guy who has a dozen good, close friends on the roster is going to have to get cut. It's a bitch. Rookies with big contracts and fat jiggling on their bodies don't get too much patience in this league.

*   *   *

He's right, and I smile every time I hear him say that stuff. I guess I sound like a veteran now, even though I'm only twenty-six, and I have told other rookies, especially the guys Lamar starts to ride, that it's tough, but it was a lot tougher for me. Bill was extensively rough on me, but he knew my college coach (defensive line coach Pete Jenkins), and he knew what I could do. It was his job to make me do it somehow, and that's what the rookies don't understand. I tell them to put up with it, to find a way to deal with Lamar, to work hard and pay attention and never lose their temper, because it won't work, it won't do at all. Nobody had it tougher than I did, not by half, and I learned a lot about myself by being able to get through it.

I sat all by myself at every meal during training camp in 1983. I was assigned to some kind of "fat man's table" while the rest of the team sat around together and walked back and forth to the buffet tables as often as they wanted. There were piles of steaks, roasted chicken, extra-thick hamburgers, and I was eating cottage cheese, fresh fruits and fresh vegetables. Man, that was rough, really rough. I just love to eat. I love fried chicken, and gumbo, and pizza. At school we used to have "eat-outs" sometime: a bunch of us would get together and order pizza on top of pizza on top of pizza. I don't eat as much as I'd like to now, because I just don't do it, but if I let myself go, I'd be like The Refrigerator, just a fat guy trying to play football.

People were also assigned to watch me, to make sure I didn't sneak out at night and bring back sacks of Big Macs or Whoppers. I did that sometimes, but not often, not when I finally understood what they expected of me. For a long time I just didn't understand. I thought it was all child's play, and although you have to be somewhat of a child to play this game, you can't act like one. It took me a long time to realize that. And a lot of pain, too. It got to a point where I went to practice one day and decided to hit anything and everything that moved. That's when I knew I was getting into the football mentality I needed, the way I should have been when I reported.

But there were other things bothering me that rookie summer, keeping me from concentrating on my job. I had been married—unwisely, I see now—at age nineteen. I had been married for about a year, and it was a bad experience because there were a lot of things about Janice I really didn't know. Even before Parcells drafted me, he took me aside and told me about marriage—about how a wife should respect me, take care of me, honor me, not spend all my money, and learn to take care of priorities. Janice and I didn't agree on what her role should be. I don't think she met my needs, and we soon separated, and finally divorced.

In the meantime, everything just piled up, kept me from sleeping. There were times when I felt it just wasn't worth it, that maybe I should quit the game and stop having people yell at me and insult me and make fun of me. I wouldn't have to work so damned hard. It was a really bad time when it should have been nothing but fun and satisfaction. I even talked about it with Bill and Lamar once, and that was good because it started me thinking in the right direction. And I can prove it, because when you read about my present wife, Annette, you'll see how smart I was to marry her.

Another invaluable source of help during these troubled times came from Dr. Joel Goldberg, a psychologist who screens prospective employees for large corporations and advises the Giants on the emotional stability of guys they are considering drafting and why certain personalities won't fit in with the chemistry of the team. He also counsels the veterans on careers, because more and more players these days are starting to realize that you have to get ready for life after football. Joel told me that veterans don't understand that pro football is an avocation, not a vocation, that something else is going to have to be part of their lives, and damned soon.

Dr. Goldberg was a great help to me, as he has been to lots of others on the team. I think it was George Young, the general manager, who decided to hire him. It was a great idea. I talked with Dr. Goldberg a lot that summer, and I finally realized that football was what I really wanted: the chance for a career. I had to get my life back in order again and find my priorities. I had to train to get back into condition and then play to be the best. But listen, I wasn't that overweight. I mean, when you talk about a guy going higher than 300 pounds, a man exceeding 310 pounds, that's fat. Look at William Perry, The Refrigerator. There's a guy who went from being able to play football at a considerable weight to a balloon trying to play football. When I reported to the Giants, I was only eight pounds over playing weight, but I wasn't in condition to play football and that made me look a lot heavier. There's a big difference. I didn't know what it really took to compete as a pro. Now I know. But it was tough, very tough, and most of it was my fault. I admit that. In the three years that I've spent working with Johnny Parker, who has gotten to be a real good friend, I know what it means to be in pro football condition.

The NFL is like an all-star game every week, you're playing the best guys at their position every game. If I had stayed in the kind of shape I started out in, I'd have been long gone by now. I'd probably have been a welder or a shipbuilder, like my daddy back home in Franklin, if I hadn't gone to college and there was no way my family could have afforded to pay my way. But I knew college was the only way out for me, and I had already started to put money away in high school, in case nobody offered me a scholarship.

But I did go, and even if I had quit the Giants, I'd have been better prepared for going into some kind of business.

I'm really glad things worked out. I know how lucky I am, and I spend a lot of time trying to give something back for all my good luck. When I was growing up it dawned on me that most of the people donating money to those ads for the United Negro College fund were Jewish people. They always understood the importance of an education, and there were a lot of Jewish families in Franklin, Louisiana. I remember Mr. Silverman and Mr. Goldstein and Mr. Wormser, business people. They'd see me in the street and say, "Hey, Leonard, nice game last week," and slip me a five-dollar bill, or a ten. I remember when I was twelve, we went to the national Biddie Basketball Tournament. It was being held in New Orleans, so a lot of people from Franklin showed up and one of the Jewish guys gave me a twenty. Man, I had never seen a twenty, much less had one, so I took all my friends and bought us hamburgers and hot dogs, about three rounds each. I don't think we played real good that night.

Before the draft that year, the Giants had invited a lot of guys to come to the stadium, to have physicals, to meet the coaches. They invited me, and I remember showing up in a New York-style cab driver's hat, denim overalls and a Giant T-shirt they had sent me. I walked into the locker room and there was Parcells with a big ear-to-ear grin on his face. "Holy shit," he said, "look at the size of this one. Who are you? Are you Marshall? Come here, Leonard, I want to talk to you." So we sat down, and you know, considering the things he said to me, if I had listened to him then it probably would have helped me mature much earlier in my career. We talked about things like marriage and commitment, about finance, about the lifestyle here so close to New York, about drugs, about things you have to do to take care of yourself and your business, as a player and as a private person. Things that a father might say to his son, which is the way he treated me when I first got here. I respected him a lot for that, and I care a lot about the guy.

Parcells had his problems, too, during that 1983 season, which was his first year as the Giant head coach and almost his last, because the record was 3–12–1 and the executives weren't too happy. And one of the main causes of that terrible season was drug-related. Cocaine mostly, that and pot (marijuana). You can probably make some guess about which guys were doing stuff by just looking at the roster the next year and the year after, and figuring out which ones were gone, guys who could still play football but no way could they play for Bill Parcells anymore.

But even though the Giants did well in not exposing these players, there was one guy whose problem was just so bad it went public. That was Malcolm Scott, who was a rookie tight end that season and who had been a fifth-round pick. Malcolm and I had been teammates at LSU. And friends. I don't think that Malcolm had any drug problems in college, not even one drug experience. I always knew him to be a very clean kid, who never had any more than a couple of beers. If anything, Malcolm liked the women. He was a ladies' man, a good-looking guy who enjoyed the night life, and I think that became his problem. I think he got to enjoy it too much. He ran into some bad people, who introduced him to other bad people, and it became a circle of bad people. Then he introduced them to other guys on the team, and I think, I don't know for sure, he dragged a couple of them into what he was doing, and that's probably why a few of them aren't here anymore.

Malcolm was my friend, though, and I felt I had to try to help. The Giants released him prior to the next season, and didn't try to hide the fact that the problem was drug-related. Even though he had showed great talent and ability as a rookie, they felt there was no place and no future for such a player in their organization.

I invited Malcolm back up here the next year. I had

known him a long time, and I cared about him and his family. I helped him to get a job up here. Through my agent, Ken Wirth, we got him an apartment, a rental car, furniture for his apartment and a membership to a health club. He worked for a substance-abuse center in Jersey City, where we got him involved in speaking to high school and junior high school kids, even elementary school kids.

He went to drug-awareness meetings, drunk-driver programs, leukemia society affairs, different things to keep his mind distracted from drugs. But for some reason Malcolm went back to it. I could never figure it out, and the people who were working with him, who were so positive and so supportive, couldn't figure it out, either. We all tried so hard, and he just went back to it.

I talked to some people last year, after Malcolm had tried out with the Saints, guys I had played with at LSU, like Hokie Gajan, Dalton Hilliard, and Eric Martin. They all thought he was having a great camp and would make the team. The next thing I knew he had been cut. Nobody knew why, so by putting two and two together, I felt it must have been drugs. I just can't understand it, he has so much talent.

I suppose I am mature enough to recognize guys who aren't. I don't blame the atmosphere or the bad guys or the fact that young guys, a lot of them from rural backgrounds, are suddenly put into a major metropolitan area with too much money in their hands. It's the maturity, or the immaturity, of the players themselves that determines the direction they take. What you want out of life determines what you'll be. If you believe in yourself, surround yourself with positive people who are go-getters, doers, guys who make it happen, you're on the right track. There's a guy out there who'll tell you he can take a dollar and make it ten. There's another guy who'll tell you he can take a dollar and make it a dollar twenty-five, a dollar-fifty.

Who's the safer guy to deal with? You never know, but you do know who's the most conservative. I'll go with the guy who can make a dollar twenty-five, a dollar-fifty. Those are the kind of guys you have to pick.

Malcolm's problems helped me in a way. Football became the most important thing to me again. Even when I was a little boy, I knew I was going to be a pro football player. My daddy says I was so strong-willed and convinced about what I wanted to be that he wouldn't argue with me. I'd sit in front of the television set and see all those great defensive linemen and just know I'd be there with them one day. I was a Pittsburgh Steeler fan—Mean Joe Greene was my favorite—but there were so many others I admired, and all I wanted was the chance to be one of them. My daddy was a Dallas Cowboy fan, and we'd root and yell at each other and, man, those Super Bowls, that was heaven.

But if there's one thing I resent about pro football, it's that I wasn't a first-round draft choice. I felt I was a lot better than other people thought, and I was drafted behind two other defensive linemen I knew I was better than. One of them is paralyzed now (Gabriel Rivera of the Pittsburgh Steelers, injured in an auto accident), and the other is in Atlanta (Mike Pitts), and I know I'm better than he is. To this day I don't know why I wasn't a first-rounder.

It gnaws at me because part of Leonard Marshall is the pursuit of wealth, and I won't try to deny that. The financial implications of being drafted in the second round cost me money, a lot of it. I figure the difference between being drafted where I was compared to the same spot in the first round cost me $500,000, maybe more. I would have gotten a $500,000 signing bonus, a stronger six-figure salary, and the chance when I negotiated my second contract to get a lot more than I am getting now. I'd probably be making the money I deserve to make.

Sure, I'm just a big country boy from Louisiana, and I'm just glad to be here. But some things are pretty obvious: I've been a starter for three years, and the last two of those I've been named to play in the Pro Bowl. And I have been a part of a Super Bowl championship team.

George Young once shed some light on that draft. He said the Giants had given me a first-round grade, but there was some question about my height. Now, while you wouldn't think that 6–3 is too short, most defensive ends are at least two inches taller. It doesn't sound like much, but the teams and their scouts think it makes a difference because the offensive tackles we go up against are usually 6–5, 6–6, even taller. In fact, George said the Giants had me ranked slightly ahead of another defensive lineman who went later in that second round, Mike Charles of Syracuse. I suppose if I had already been drafted, they might have considered taking Charles, but from what I know, he has been erratic, kind of a disappointment, and recently somebody said he had been fined and suspended because of some drug thing. Mike Charles? Mike Charles was ranked as good as me? It just doesn't make sense.

CHAPTER 2

TAYLOR AND BURT: LAYING IT ON THE LINE

"The guys next door, you know?"

There are at least two guys to keep in mind when considering how well, or how badly, I have played in any given game—Jim Burt and Lawrence Taylor.

Burt is the nose tackle. (Some people call his position nose guard, others middle guard.) The New York Giants' defense features a three-man front line. With only three players on the line, two are ends, one on either side. Last season, when we won Super Bowl XXI in Pasadena, the ends were George Martin on the left and me on the right. The guy between us was the nose tackle, Jim Burt. (You remember Jim Burt. He's the one who jumped into the stands after we won the National Conference championship by shutting out the Washington Redskins, slapped some high-fives with the faithful, then jumped back down to the field and danced his way into the locker room.)

With the use of the currently popular three-man defensive front, what is simply referred to as the 3–4 defense calls for three linemen up front and four linebackers behind them.

Two of the four are outside linebackers and the other

two play inside, so obviously, you can't have a middle linebacker in a four-man set. But one of the linebackers is critical to the way I play and to the things I'm able to do. That's Lawrence Taylor, the right outside linebacker.

When Burt does his job properly, which most of the time means occupying at least two offensive linemen—the center and a guard—I have the luxury of going up against a single offensive lineman, usually the tackle. When I am man-to-man against one guy, I am going to win that war. When they start double-teaming me and holding me and stuff like that, things get a lot more difficult. So I need Jim to keep those guys off me.

When it started to look like the two best pass rushers on the great Giant defense were Lawrence Taylor and myself, head coach Bill Parcells did a strange thing—strange, that is, to those who don't understand the intricacies of defense: He put us on the same side of the defense.

Why would he put his best quarterback snuffers on one side, next to each other? Why not put one on the left side, one on the right, and make the offense stop us coming in from two directions?

To coach Parcells it was simple. If I'm on the right side and L. T. is on the left, both of us are going to be double-teamed. That means we can both be blocked. Neutralized. But on the same side, who's gonna block both of us? Are teams gonna put four guys on blocking duty for just two of our guys? No, sir. So we give them a choice. They can work hard and stop me, or they can work hard and stop Lawrence. But we don't think they can stop us both.

You know what? For the last three years Parcells has been absolutely right. The strategy worked. Last year, Lawrence led the league with 20½ sacks. I was fourth, with 12.

Lawrence had his problems before the season started, and everybody knew how hard he was trying to overcome them. I told him we both were going to have a great season because we were going to help each other and, together, no offense in this league was good enough to stop us. I think every guy on the team rallied around L. T. Hey, he made a mistake. His life-style is his choice and sometimes I don't agree with it, but he's a teammate, a friend and one of our best players. He deserved our support, and I think he needed it, too.

Burt's defensive role is less important unless the offense we're playing against chooses to stop me with the left guard and left tackle. That forces the offensive blocking scheme to either (1) have the center handle Burt one-on-one, (2) keep a running back "at home" in the backfield, or (3) pull over the right guard to help the center with Burt. That would allow George Martin to play one-on-one with the right tackle. And remember, until the 1986 season-ending injury to defensive end Curtis McGriff, George was the Giants' designated pass rusher in sure passing situations.

So you can see the problem the three of us create. Lawrence Taylor, Jim Burt and I can do a lot of damage to an offensive blocking scheme. Lawrence, of course, has become a legendary linebacker. Yet in reality he may not be the best all-around linebacker the Giants have. I think our best is Carl Banks, the Giants' left outside linebacker. But in terms of what he is asked to do—and what the fans want him to do—Lawrence is more exciting and can more quickly disrupt a game. He is a pass rusher of awesome skill, the best there is—maybe the best ever—at rushing the passer from a linebacker's position.

Even so—and Lawrence may not like this—I would say that he is really a "stand up" defensive end who takes a position on the line of scrimmage to my outside, or right. Technically, that makes me a defensive tackle in a four-man front. Lawrence has great power and strength, unusual speed and quickness for a man who stands 6–3 and weighs 245. But in all the other, less spectacular things a linebacker has to do, I think Banks is better. He just isn't as dramatic, as crowd pleasing, as glamorous as the man who crushes the quarterback.

Talking to a large group of sportswriters during the week before the Super Bowl, Lawrence described what a perfect sack means to him. "Well, you see, the best kind of sack is when he [the quarterback] doesn't know I'm coming in, doesn't know I've beaten the last blocker and have a clear shot. Especially when he's looking downfield, the other side of the field, waiting for the receiver to make that last get-clear move, you know? He's not even aware of me, his back is to me and I can really nail him. That's when I raise up just a little, to be able to get him right in the back, and I kind of uncoil when I make contact, drilling him right between the shoulder blades. When he's on the ground and has dropped the ball and is just lying there, eyes glazed, snot oozing from his nose and mouth, his teammates coming over to see if he's still breathing—that's when I know I have made a perfect sack."

Lawrence is a little intense. He is also a little unpredictable. He made headlines in February 1986 when he checked himself into a clinic in Texas that specializes in treating those with a chemical dependency. Last spring, Lawrence finally admitted it was cocaine.

L. T. has also been known to enjoy himself, and he has never attempted to hide that. He is a larger-than-life character, an athlete more gifted than any I've ever seen, a once-in-a-generation specimen who likes pushing himself to new physical limits.

I like Lawrence, but I couldn't live the way he does. Lawrence is a very sheltered person who doesn't like a lot of people around him. He doesn't let people get close to him. He loves that sheltered life-style when dealing with the other players. He's got a few friends among the players he's usually with, but ninety percent of his friends are not players. But even though he's cool toward the players, a lot of guys still respect him and his abilities. What other guy do you know who can go from flat on his back to NFL Player of the Year in one season?

I don't think Lawrence thinks much about himself, but he's concerned with what other people think of him, what other people perceive him to be. I think he would much rather other people think of him as Lawrence the Great, you know, instead of Lawrence Taylor the person.

Before George Young got here and hired Ray Perkins as head coach in 1979, before he hired Bill to replace him in 1983, Alex Webster and later John McVay were the head coaches. Things were a little relaxed, from what I've heard, in the locker room and at meetings. Players used to talk during meetings, used to bring sandwiches and drinks in with them. Then they'd have seasons like 4–12. Bill Parcells wouldn't ever stand for stuff like that. You do that, you're gone. Right away. Discipline—that's what makes winning teams. A player like Taylor might not be as dominant as he is if that velvet-glove attitude had remained. In fact, L.T.'s problems probably would have become magnified and maybe even ended his career.

Anyway, I still think Carl Banks just might be a better all-around linebacker than Lawrence. I think he's more consistent against the pass. I don't think Lawrence is bothered by that, because he knows the kind of player he has been, but he also knows there's always another great player who comes around and is recognized, and now it's Carl's turn. But if Lawrence continues to work at the game the way other young players are working at it, then he will continue to be the type of dominating player he already is. Keep in mind that he's already accomplished a lot of things Carl has yet to accomplish. Lawrence Taylor is endowed with a talent that many players wish they had, and if he cherishes it, he can keep it for a long time.

I recognized that kind of athletic ability in myself at a

much younger age. I knew it was something special, something in the way I moved, in how I was able to do certain things so easily. But God wouldn't let me keep it for long. It's gone now, and while I know I am an excellent athlete, that special thing, that quality you recognize deep within yourself and try to cherish . . . man, it's gone. Lawrence Taylor still has it. God let him keep it into his adult years. It is a very special gift from God, and if he cherishes it and holds onto it for a long time, he'll always be a great athlete.

For his sake, I hope he becomes more of a team guy, because he's a likable person. I mean, you can't dislike Lawrence Taylor. A lot of people wouldn't like to have the life-style he has, and he gets criticized, sure he does, but remember, he's under a lot of pressure. He's renowned as the greatest player on the Giants, the greatest player in football, and that's a terrible burden to carry. Certain types of people are attracted to him, guys who maybe aren't the nicest people in the world, guys interested in the money and the good times and the fast-lane kind of life.

It's tough to weed through all the bullshit, and some guys never do. It's hard to say if L. T. has that problem because I'm not around him enough. But I've been around. I met some very bad people when I lived in Harmon Cove Towers, when I lived in Jersey City, when I lived in Rutherford. They're all over. They come around to the money, the athlete, the celebrity, and they offer a whole new way of life: a world of drug people, fast women, fast money, going into New York City and doing things you've only dreamed about.

In my own way, I've become a kind of observer of some of our players, and I've been able to recognize some interesting and satisfying changes. Take Perry Williams, our starting right cornerback. When he first came here he never said a word, never spoke to anybody. Now, four years later, you can't get him to shut up. Banks was like that, too, wouldn't say a thing to anybody, and now he talks more than Lamar Leachman. And when you talk more than Lamar, that's really saying something.

Several other guys have also changed. Zeke Mowatt, a real quiet kid from rural Florida, has opened up a little—at first he never said a thing to anybody. Andy Headen came here running around and doing his own thing. Now he's trying to settle down a little, leave here with something tangible. There are guys I've seen who I thought were headed bad, but who turned it around.

Drugs, racism, special treatment—if it's not one kind of pressure, it's another. It's all part of the pro football experience. But for the blacks, the problem is usually racist, which comes up in unexpected ways. I tell you what blew my mind last season. We got a letter at the stadium from a black guy—first time I'd ever seen anything like it—about the Howard Beach incident, when a black kid got killed by a gang of whites in an all-white section of Queens. The guy said that all the Giants, "all you brothers," were just house niggers. He said we should boycott the championship game against the Redskins because of how the white people were treating the brothers up here. It was the same shit as what used to go on in Georgia and Mississippi and Alabama and Louisiana, he said, and we shouldn't let it go on, that the whites think they're down south and that "you guys just aren't together."

Harry Carson read the letter over the intercom in the locker room. We laughed at it—we knew where it, where the guy, was coming from. There's never been a black–white thing here. Even at LSU it never really happened. We'd go out drinking together and a black guy would introduce a black chick to a white guy, or a white guy would introduce a white chick to a black guy. But there were a lot of people who didn't like it, and who wouldn't like it up here, either. In that respect it's easier here, because black and white is more common. But there's more pressure on celebrities, on sports stars, because more people try to pattern their life-styles after you, want to be identified with you.

That's a problem in general. They want your autograph, want to be in a picture with you; there's just so many people that you can't get away from it. It's difficult, sometimes it's a pain in the ass, but those are the people who buy the tickets, read the papers, listen to the talk shows, and when they stop paying attention, then you start to worry.

So Lawrence Taylor was in a drug rehabilitation program, and fourteen months later he admitted it to a high school assembly at his alma mater in Williamsburg, Virginia. It was said that the preliminary treatment that was breaking him of his dependency went real quick, but I don't think anyone will ever know what it must have cost in pain.

When Bill Parcells first heard about it, people tell me he was really angry, wanted to trade Lawrence because he had lied to him about drugs, but he calmed down and then became very protective of him. Bill wouldn't talk with any of the sportswriters who are always hanging around the team—sure it's their job, I know that, but sometimes they're a pain in the ass. Bill wouldn't answer any questions about L. T. except about football subjects. He told them that if they bothered him with those kind of questions he'd close the locker rooms, and bar all of them from the daily access to the players. I don't know if he could have gotten away with that, but he was really serious.

Later in camp, he repeated his threat. This time he made it personal, saying, "The next guy who asks me about Lawrence Taylor's problem is gonna have trouble getting out of his chair." I don't think any of the writers took him up on it.

I'm sure glad L. T. got over that problem, because he's the most important player on the team in terms of what I do, and vice versa. I do some things that make those sacks come for him, and when he's hot there's no way they are going to stop me, too. We have a good rapport. Sometimes during a game we even do things on the field that the coaches aren't expecting. We'll do little deals, tricks—I'll go outside and he'll come inside, you know? Usually those things work, because we're in the game and we know what the other team is trying to do. We do things our own way, we ad lib a lot. We'll talk during the week and try to figure out what we can do to create a situation, to disrupt their offense, to put the quarterback off rhythm. Often when we see how the offensive line is playing us, we'll run a lot of "games" and sometimes I'll do things with Jim (Burt) inside.

When we change things, it drives Bill Parcells crazy. We take a chance when we do it, but as long as we make it work, he can't bitch about it too much. During the playoffs our defense went through an overhaul. I had no other responsibilities in those games except to go a hundred miles an hour on every play, try to get the quarterback, crush the running back in the backfield. No other responsibilities. I liked that. It was all-out pass rush regardless of down and distance, and yes, it was a little risky, but it sure surprised the hell out of a lot of guys.

They changed L. T.'s role, too. They moved him around, used him a little in pass coverage, even though when he does that he isn't as effective because pass coverage just isn't his cup of tea. He wants to rush the passer, and that's what he does best. When he's in pass coverage, he isn't contributing as much as when he's on the line of scrimmage. But if he was a defensive end, his pass rush wouldn't be that effective. He's too light, for one thing. He's under 250. Many of the tackles are 280, 290, even more. But when Lawrence gets a head start, he can use his quickness, start from different places and get everybody upset because they don't know where he's coming from.

But L. T.'s drug problem, despite his life-style, came as a surprise to me and to most of the Giants. He came from the same kind of family I did. A strong family, good parents. But I guess he was hanging out with some people who weren't right for him, who led him into things he wasn't ready to deal with. He told that high school class that part of the problem was too much money in his pocket and not enough ideas of what to do with it. I worry about the effect of his reputation on impressionable kids. I think about kids a lot, and I know they see that he got away with something wrong, and it's a problem for me. If there's just one or two kids out there who I can help, who think I mean something to them, then I want to do everything I can to get them away from the wrong stuff, the drugs and the bad life. I worry about it a lot, and I'm very concerned with how kids perceive me. I want to be recognized as a guy who lived a good, clean life, who gave something back to the league, the sport and the community. I don't want to be the big sports star who makes millions of dollars and hangs out with the rich white people—and the rich blacks—and doesn't give a damn about the real people, the ones who need help, the ones who are growing up the way I did, and worse, who don't think anything good is ever going to happen for them.

I try to be the right kind of role model to kids, especially inner-city kids. I feel I can help a lot with poor black kids. I understand their problem, I know where they're coming from. Drugs and alcohol are crutches, from constant depression because they can't have the things they want, so they do what they can to turn on. There are kids who will never get out of where they are, who can't play a sport, who won't become doctors, lawyers, corporation executives, who will never make big, big money. If they ask me,

"What should I do, Mr. Marshall?" I tell them education. Educate through the streets and the schools. Find a trade, find something and use it as a stepping-stone to something better. Take advantage of the school system and the teachers, of their families, their real friends. Don't build a life on negatives like drugs, alcohol, gangs, crime, beating on whites, on cops. Build with positive things, maybe reach higher than they think they should. Hey, always reach for the moon. What else is there?

People say I'm an entrepreneur, a twenty-six-year-old tycoon trying to reach my goal of becoming a millionaire without counting on my football salary. So why not? Shouldn't I want what's best for me, for Annette? Shouldn't I want what I think is attainable? You know, what L. T. said, that he had too much money—man, there's no such thing, you never have too much money. He said sometimes he had six, seven thousand dollars in his pocket? Well, there's a damned good place for it and it starts with a B and stands for bank. It sure doesn't start with an N for nose. And if he can't put it in a bank, put it in a safe in his house, take his friends out to dinner, set up a college fund for a poor kid who doesn't have any money, buy a piece of property. You can never be too well off. We athletes have a chance to make things good later on. Whether it's fair or not I won't judge, but we have the opportunity. It's a crime to waste it.

Jim Burt, the guy the writers call Sluggo, is a different kind of player. He is almost immune to pain, or seems that way. He was determined to succeed against all odds, and he did, an undrafted player who signed with the Giants as a free agent after the 1981 draft. The teams picked over three hundred players, and nobody thought Jim Burt was good enough to be one of them, even though he made a few All-America teams as a nose guard when he played for the University of Miami in Florida. You'd think somebody would have taken a chance.

George Young did. He quickly contacted the undrafted Burt. The Giants had an advantage because of George's friendship with Howard Schnellenberger, Miami's head coach at the time. He apparently told Burt that George Young was "good people" and that he'd be treated fairly. So they brought him in for a tryout two days after the draft and decided not to let him out of Giants Stadium without getting his signature on a contract. People ask why Jim wasn't drafted—after all, he was in the Pro Bowl last year. Maybe it's because he was such an overachiever nobody felt he could keep up that intense pace in this league. Also he was too short. He just didn't fit into any computers, didn't agree with anybody's definition of a pro nose tackle. Remember, the position is still sort of new. There aren't many rules, no guidebooks to help the scouts determine a "natural" nose tackle. The teams going to the 3–4 defense simply created the position, and now the colleges have to groom players to fill it.

I think there's a trend now that nose tackles don't have to be very tall, which is good because Jim Burt isn't. He's barely 6–1. But coaches want their nose tackles to be very strong, and Jim Burt is that and more. And they must have a peculiar twist in their personalities to enjoy being in the middle, where bigger, maybe even stronger men are attacking their knees, where there's head butting, forearm shots, fists swinging. Bill Parcells says that guys who play the nose tackle position shouldn't be too well adjusted. Why? So they won't know what's happening. If they had any brains at all, do you think they'd agree to be nose tackles? That's really great for Jim Burt, because well adjusted he's not.

Burt is one of Parcells' favorites. It was Burt, not linebacker Harry Carson, who started pouring the Gatorade bucket on Parcells, and it's possible that no other player could have gotten away with it. More important, it was Jim Burt who did something to Parcells that only he could have gotten away with. When he was a rookie, the Giants were playing an exhibition game, and Burt didn't start. But Bill told him he might get in. Parcells was a defensive assistant coach then. Well, the game started and suddenly somebody crashes into Parcells from behind, knocks him down. It was Burt. He had chopped him with a forearm. Nobody else on this team could have gotten away with that. It is one of my beliefs that you don't have to like everybody on your team in order to play well, but you can get along with people well without really liking them. There are things about Jim Burt I don't really appreciate. Since I arrived here, he has seemed to be a guy searching for identity, looking for a way to establish character, a way to establish respect from the other players. He's caught up in this ego thing about being a free agent and not a drafted football player. He was trying to find a way to gain respect not only from his intermediate coaches like Lamar Leachman and the rest of the guys around him, but from the whole organization.

But he was trying to do it by being egotistical, not by being himself—although maybe that is himself, to live a life of trying to impress people. It's not a matter of me liking him or not, it's more a case of his ego being so big and me not wanting to deal with it. I don't dislike Jim Burt, I just don't appreciate some parts of his personality.

Would it have been the same if I had been the one who jumped into the stands? Would I have gotten all that instant notoriety? I wouldn't have done it, it just isn't me. Besides, the Northeast is a little different. It's not exactly racism, you see, it's an ethnic thing. There are a lot of Irish people here, and Burt's Irish and they love him. There are a lot more of them than blacks.

Jim Burt is 6–1 and weighs 260. I was thought to be a little too short for defensive end, but I'm 6–3, which is

perfect nose tackle height, and I am at least as quick as
Burt even though I outweigh him by at least 25 pounds. I
am as strong as he is, too. In some ways, other than weight-
lifting. I'm stronger. I'm a stronger inside pass rusher,
my lateral movement is a little bit better and there are
some things I can do better because of my natural ability
as an athlete. If we were both nose tackles on the Giants?
I'd have to say that if it came down to blood or draw, it'd
be my job.

I could play nose tackle. If I was asked to, if I had to do
it for a living, I'm sure I could play nose tackle for the
Giants. Why not? It wouldn't matter if I liked it, it just
wouldn't matter. If I had to play the position, I'd do it well.
I'm sure of that.

In fact, I also think I could have been a National Football League quality linebacker. If I played at 260, I
think I could stand in there. I'd have to be an inside
linebacker, and I could pound it with the best of them. I
could drop back and play pass coverage, too, I'm sure of it.
In fact, I think I could have been the player I feel Pepper
Johnson, a rookie linebacker last year, is going to be. But I
never talked to Parcells about it. I'm a defensive end and
I'm doing all right and I don't think it's the right time to
make that kind of drastic change.

Although recently I did talk to coach about a different
position. I talked to Ray Handley, our offensive backfield
coach, right before the Super Bowl. Why? I wanted to run
with the ball in the Super Bowl like The Refrigerator did
the year before. But mostly I'm concerned with the respect of the other players on the team, at least in the
context of rifts that can be damaging to the overall team
camaraderie. It's not good when you have egos clashing.
Look at the Chicago Bears. They weren't successful this
past season because they had ego problems with their
quarterbacks. Jim McMahon, their starter the year before
who missed most of the season with an injured shoulder,

seemed to feel his role with the team was to be a butt-head both on and off the field. And if anybody else got put in the quarterback position, to be a butt-head to that person, as Doug Flutie found out.

From talking to other Bear players, some of whom I've gotten to know personally, there was a good deal of ego-clashing among McMahon, Flutie and coach Mike Ditka. They had a less than successful season, and I think the ego thing was one of the reasons. It was just so distracting. I know it would be if that kind of thing happened here. Do the Giants have that kind of a situation? Is it possible that we would be the Chicago Bears this season? Is there a dangerous mix of egos on this team?

I guess it is always a possibility where egos play a big part of what you do for a living. Most of the people we have are, well . . . it's not hard to tell which of our guys are on an ego trip. I mean, what guy in his right mind do you know who would jump into the stands and try to high-five people after a game? What guy do you know who would run out on the field and wave a towel before the game, like wide receiver Phil McConkey? I mean, there are guys who have balls as big as their bodies. People think we all knew that Burt was going to jump into the stands after the NFC championship victory over the Redskins, that it was all arranged. Nobody knew, and I'm not sure even Jim knew. I mean, Dennis Harrah, the Rams' guard, had a joke at the Pro Bowl a week after the Super Bowl. His act was like that show on television, the *Gong Show*. He put on a kind of "guess-who-I-am?" act, got on his knees and said, "What short football player in the NFL runs into the stands and tries to high-five people?" It was a joke, but that's the kind of thing that shows everyone knows who the characters are.

Do I resent it? No, sir, who am I to resent anything? I leave my game on the field, good game or bad. I want to be recognized by what I do on the field, by being a contributor to the team. You look at guys like quarterback Phil Simms, who plays solid, steady football. He earns his reputation for that. Joe Morris, same kind of player, leaves his game on the field. Those are the kind of players I want to be like. I don't want the image of a guy who had to do hot-dog stuff to get recognized.

I know that Burt's contract expired last season and that he was negotiating during the spring and summer. He's going to get more money, undoubtedly a lot more money, and he should, although I wouldn't think they'd pay him the same money they'd pay a drafted football player. I would expect them to pay him less than they pay me, sure. And if I find out different, I'll have a big gripe. Hey, I've been to the Pro Bowl twice, the only Giant defensive lineman to go twice since Jim Katcavage did it back in the Sixties. And if Jim Burt does things like jumping into the stands, it shouldn't affect how much money he gets. You should look at the numbers, the tackles and the sacks and the pressures, and at his value to the defense. I thought Jim Burt had a good season. I thought he should have gone to the Pro Bowl, and when he had those back spasms near the end of the season, I thought he hurt his chances. But he came back and played strong anyway. Yeah, I thought he had a good year.

I have pride, and I have an ego, too, and I genuinely feel that I am one of the best defensive ends in the business. Do I feel that Jim Burt is one of the two or three best nose tackles in the National Football League? I don't. I wouldn't rate him in the top two or three, but he's definitely in the top ten. No doubt. There are four guys who I think are the most ferocious nose tackles in the game today, and they're ferocious because of their size, speed and quickness inside. Joe Klecko of the Jets is the best. Second is Bill Pickel of the Raiders, then Bill Maas of Kansas City and Joe Nash of the Seattle Seahawks. I think the last three are still improving. Steve McMichael in Chicago is a great nose tackle. You'll have to put Reggie White of the Philadelphia Eagles up there with Klecko soon, because he has the size and speed and range. Last year Atlanta had a rookie, Tony Casillas, who is going to be very good.

On our team the linebackers are so good that mistakes up front can be made up without anybody noticing. A lot of teams don't have an eight-year Pro Bowl player like Harry Carson standing in the middle. Or a young 245-pound rookie like Pepper Johnson. Or a really big linebacker like Andy Headen, who's 6–5 and 245, who can't even start for us. Not to mention Carl Banks and Lawrence Taylor. A lot depends on where you are, what your role is, what your value is to the team.

An interesting thought: What if the Giants had one of those great nose tackles like Klecko, like White maybe? Would the defense be better? Would it change? Would my job become easier? No doubt. And it's going to change. The nose tackle who no doubt is going to be another Klecko is Erik Howard, who was a rookie last season and one of those four second-round draft picks we had. He bench-presses 560 pounds, squats as much as he benches and has quickness and ability. He is going to be a great football player. He has all the tools—size, speed, strength, smarts. He asks questions when he doesn't understand, talks with the players and coaches until he learns. And he has the playing mentality of a young bull. I just hope he doesn't let his ego get as big as some of these other guys, and start to think that he has life by the balls.

What does Erik's presence do to Jim Burt? I would think it weakens his position, his negotiating power. When you're faced with competition that has that much talent, it makes it tough to sleep at night. Hey, I've got some reason to worry, too. They drafted a defensive end, John Washington, in the third round last year, and I have to be concerned. He's very good, very strong and quick. I keep that in mind, but I have to feel my position isn't as threatened as Jim Burt's, you know? The Giants know what they have in me.

Do I like Jim Burt? I know I respect him. I admire his toughness and dedication and ability. But is there a feeling of friendship and camaraderie between us? I don't know, I could be wrong, but I think he feels like he deserves more than I do. And if he does, that's his problem. I don't deal with a lot of people for that reason. I think if Jim Burt didn't depend so much on his ego, he'd be a really great person.

The week before the Super Bowl he made a childish remark about me, something he shouldn't have said. I think he just wanted to embarrass me. That I shouldn't be here, that I was a fat piece of garbage, that I ran just two laps in the mile we had to do when I first got here. Which shows he doesn't know what the hell he's talking about because I ran a lot more than that. And other crap: like they kept me here because I was a high draft choice, kept me around when they shouldn't have. I think he's really insulted that he wasn't a drafted football player. He was a paperback All-America at Miami. So I was drafted, came here overweight, got a lot of money. And he wasn't even drafted. He really let me know that this big jealousy trip had built up inside of him.

Sure, I said things back to him. I said they should have cut his ass, he's too short to play, that he owes the world to Bill Parcells. I talked a lot with Gary Jeter when I first got here, even though he had been traded. He knew a lot about the personalities of the team, who was doing what with whom. He told me a lot about the defensive linemen especially, about all the cliques that were set up around here, and that I shouldn't get involved. I asked him questions about Lamar, what kind of coach he was, what he liked, stuff like that. He told me Lamar was a good guy, most of the other players were, too, but he also told me to watch out for Jim Burt.

When people ask me about Jim Burt in public, I don't like to respond. We get along on the field, in the locker room, but I don't think I could get along with him socially.

He's the only guy on the team I ever had a problem with. I dress next to Brad Benson, L. T. and Harry Carson, all of us Pro Bowl players, and I get along with them and everybody else. L. T. is a totally different kind of guy, he horses around, he may tease, say a few things. Harry, too. But it's never the kind of issue that could trigger your temper into a fight. The only guy I ever had that kind of problem with was Burt. When we play, we're next to each other, and we do it because it's our job. Hey, if I don't do it, I'm outta here. We even say things to each other, like "nice hit," but it's just two guys working together because we have to.

I think: Sure, it would be better for me if Erik Howard wins the job this year. I don't think it'll be any different on the field, but I'm quite sure that if Erik beats out Burt for the job, it will put things in a better perspective. I help Erik a lot, but that's not because I'm trying to help him with his job. I'm just trying to be fair. Hell, I take time and try to help John Washington, and he's the end behind me who I figure is gonna take my job someday.

When I was a rookie, everybody was worried about their own jobs, nobody would help me at all. Well, George Martin was helpful, but other guys like Dee Hardison just left me alone, let me learn what I could from the coaches or by watching. But nobody was very helpful or open about showing the rookie what things were all about. So I try not to act like that because I remember how much of a pain it was, how hurt I was.

I'm not sure I like the way this reads. I don't want to hurt Burt's feelings, and I don't want to come off sounding like some team spokesman who thinks it's his job to watch over everybody. I'm not that way. I'm really a big, easygoing guy who loves what he does and shows up for work every day happy and looking forward to it. How many guys out there feel the same way about their jobs? People are probably going to mistake some of the things I say, but I can't help but speak what's on my mind, how I feel. It's hard for me not to voice an opinion, and with Jim Burt, I guess you have to say I do like him, and yet there are things about him I don't like, too. It's a lot like real life, like the personal interactions in business, and I am a businessman. I'll be involved in business for the rest of my life, long after football is gone.

CHAPTER 3

"I'm lookin' at earning over two-and-half million, maybe more, just from football in the next six years."

FOOTBALL AND MONEY

Significantly more money is earned by players in major league baseball than in pro football. This is not to say, however, that pro football players are living anywhere near striking distance of poverty. They average—and there are more than 1,500 of them on salary—better than $220,000 a year. Such quarterbacks as Jim Kelly of Buffalo, Dan Marino of Miami and rookie Vinny Testaverde of Tampa Bay earn more than a million bucks a year. For throwing a football. Herschel Walker of the Dallas Cowboys is in that elite neighborhood, and so is Walter Payton of the Chicago Bears, Eric Dickerson of the Los Angeles Rams and Mark Gastineau of the New York Jets.

The Giants' Lawrence Taylor commands a gross salary of $900,000 a year; their quarterback, Phil Simms, can count on $850,000. All of these figures are for straight salary, and don't begin to include incentive bonuses, playoff money and all the off-the-field, out-of-season money for commercials, endorsements and guest appearances, much of that coming in the form of pocketable cash. But there are iniquities nevertheless, generally defined by position.

Defensive backs make less than offensive linemen, who make less than defensive linemen, who make less than linebackers, who make less than running backs, who make less than quarterbacks. But within the categories, there are further injustices. Ask Leonard Marshall, who ranks approximately fiftieth down the list of defensive linemen in the league in terms of salary.

My contract with the Giants is fair, given that I'm the highest paid lineman with the exception of George Martin. But in terms of league salaries, I just don't get paid the way a guy who has been to the last two Pro Bowls should. I'm convinced I should make more, especially when I look around the NFL and see what other guys who play my position are taking home. I look at guys like Dwaine Board and Michael Carter of the Forty-Niners, Richard Dent and Dan Hampton of the Bears, Howie Long of the Raiders, Bob Golic of the Browns. I can go on down the line and name guys who have been in this league no longer than I have, some not even as long, and they're making hundreds of thousands of dollars more than I am. For instance, I think I'm as good a player as Mark Gastineau of the New York Jets is, but he gets a lot more ink and a lot more money. I think I'm as valuable to my club. Look, I like Mark as a player and as a person, and I think we're good friends and fans of each other, but I just don't understand why he makes more money than I do. I guess it's because he's had more quarterback sacks in his eight or nine years than I've had in my four.

For what I do, as a leader and a player, I feel I should be making more. A lot more. All I hear is that George Young says there isn't enough money for big raises and he can't justify giving every player a raise when he asks because he has to watch a salary scale. I know what he's doing, it's what any businessman would do. He's trying to save as much of the company's money as he can. I appreciate that. I understand that. I would be trying to do the same thing, to save my company as much money as possible. But you have to keep in mind that this is a young team with only a few guys over thirty years old, guys like Harry Carson, George Martin, Brad Benson, Tony Galbreath . . . I think Simms is just thirty. We are going to be good for a long time, and if we keep winning our salaries are going to have to keep going up, and pretty soon he's going to have to tear up his salary scale and make up a new one. In a lot of ways, the Giants are great to work for. They try to make your life easier; they make it easy to get tickets; they help when they can, like with job counseling, setting up a college program nearby at Fairleigh Dickinson University so the guys who didn't graduate can become part-time students and get their degrees. Quality-of-life things. But in other ways, little ways, certain attitudes, they're just annoying. I guess it's like that working for any big company. If everybody was one hundred percent happy all the time something would be wrong.

I am very careful, almost meticulous, with my money. My financial advisor, who is also my agent, is Ken Wirth of Greenwich Financial Concepts, Inc., and with his guidance I have made carefully considered investments. Ken and I joined forces to build a solid financial base for me—both on and off the field. I've come a long way, and I'm expecting things to get better, and more fruitful, with time. Most of the money goes into real estate—office buildings, residential condominiums to rent, properties in New Jersey, New York, North Carolina and Cape Cod. I have formed my own corporation, Big Time Enterprises, Inc., and some of the money goes through there, along with some of the investments. I see all the bills, pay all the bills, write all the checks; I want to know exactly what's going on. When Ken and I decide to acquire a piece of property, we go over the prospectus clause by clause. I don't want to do anything I don't understand. I don't ever want to be the kind of athlete you read about who loses a lot of money because he didn't know what his people were doing with it. Ken is one of my closest friends. He was the best man at my wedding. But I still want to know everything that happens to my money.

Every salary check goes into our account. All of it: preseason expense checks, regular season salary checks, postseason playoff money, even the Super Bowl check I received last March. It all goes into the bank. Believe it or not, I still live like a pauper. I walk around with no more than two, three hundred dollars in my pocket. I don't like traveling with a lot of money. I like credit cards. It's helpful to my accounting people to show them how I'm spending the money, on what and why. And I never take the opportunity to pay those small option payments, you know? Every bill, no matter how big it is, gets paid at each end of the month.

I expect to play at least six more years, and I figure to earn at *least* two-and-a-half to three million dollars just for playing football. I expect to earn an additional $250,000 a year in income related to football. After football I expect that will be a minimum. We're setting up all these deals and investments now, so hopefully I won't ever have to worry about money. And that's something for a poor black kid from Franklin, Louisiana.

I remember how it was growing up, and although we weren't poor, there never was a lot of money, certainly not like now. I get a net payroll check of roughly $23,000 once a week for sixteen weeks during the season. The biggest single check I ever saw with my name on it was my bonus money when I signed on as a rookie. It was for $165,000. It was there on a piece of paper and it had my name on it. I put it right in the bank.

Oh, I have indulged myself a little. Why not? The first thing I bought was a car, the second a gold chain. I bought a 300-D Mercedes-Benz, got almost 80,000 miles on it and then sold it. But I don't mean I really bought it. I leased it with an option to buy. That way I was able to deduct the lease payments, the gas, the mileage, plus I deducted the depreciation of the car. It worked out pretty well. There are two automobiles in the Marshall family these days, and both of them are leased. One is a Mercedes-Benz 560-SL. The other is a Bronco Two. We're saving money so that in about two years we can get a nice 560-SL to match, one that I can fit into. I've found ways to enjoy my money without really spending it. I'm just trying to make sure I do everything right so that when the glitter and glamour of football is over, my future will be just as fruitful.

With football as a stepping-stone, my long range goal is to move smoothly, in a financial sense, into another career. But if this stopped right now, there's enough money to put me into something else. So I guess you can say that at a young age I've established myself comfortably, at least, for this chapter of my life. But there are unfortunately certain pitfalls for a professional athlete—sharks and barracudas, like the real ones, circling in the water, waiting for the chance to take advantage of a kid with too much money, no guidance and not enough experience to do it himself. I have met a lot of them. In the beginning I cost myself some money—no, a lot of money—because I didn't know better, because I trusted people I never even should have been associating with, people I walk away from now. But that's how you learn, I guess.

More interesting, I think, is another phenomenon: The more money you make, the more bad people you'll meet. There are just so many bad professionals out there looking for the easy score. When a black guy gets to be a name, they don't consider him to be just a black guy. All of a sudden he's a black guy with status, with a reputation— and with some cabbage in the bank. I've found people who just want to make a dollar off me. Hell, you meet these people and right away you know what's going on. They try to get too involved and too active in your money, in what you're doing with your money, what you're doing for yourself. I just don't let myself get too interested in people like that. When I'm approached by these types, I just say thanks for the opportunity, but no thanks, I'm not interested.

If they have something super and explain it to me and somebody I trust, then maybe we can do something. It's my money and my life, and I can't expect anybody else to live it for me. Even with Ken, I don't feel comfortable just letting him do it, don't bother me about the details. A money manager has to have a hundred clients to make enough money; he can't make enough just from me, or he damned well better not. I'm involved in everything we do. I go through land leases, building leases, dollar values, landlord demands, the whole bit. And I get an education. I trust Ken with everything, but I mostly trust his advice. I respect and admire Ken, and I love him as a close friend. He's provided a partnership and positive guidance and is as close to me as a big brother. But I write all the checks. I have my hands on all the money.

I'm not into doing a lot of free stuff because you get taken advantage of, but I do a lot of charity, things you feel in your heart you should do. I'm very active in the Leukemia Society, for instance. You have to be willing to give something back to the community, to show your appreciation for all the good fortune you've had, to share it somehow with those who are poor or sick or just adrift. You see, I think I'm a nice man. Truly a nice man. My heart's in the right place. I know how to help those in need. I cherish the thought of knowing I've touched someone in a special way.

But I would not insult a friend by offering him money if he was in trouble, because that's demeaning and diminishes a man's image of himself. I'll help, though. I'll use some contact to find him a job; I'll talk to a friendly banker and get him a credit line. Something constructive. I'd rather keep a friend than force somebody to pay back money they can't afford to pay back. I try to instruct the young players how important it is to control their money, how not to spend money on things that don't matter, that don't last, how to find people who have your best interests, and theirs, at heart. There are guys on this Giant team who make a lot of money—man, I mean a lot of money—who are having financial difficulties, who need cash and can't get it, who have spent it all, who continue to borrow, to spend foolishly. That'll never be Leonard Marshall, and I'm trying to show them that it never has to be them, either.

I've got plans, major plans, like trying to do financial planning one day for young players who have no one to turn to and who have been raised with an inbred distrust of people. I'd like to have all my investments working for me, but I want to do something, too. I'd like to have a chain of sporting goods franchises, a Louisiana-style restaurant up around New York, a nice Italian deli like a place I go to called Balducci's in Manhattan, everything in one place. Yeah, I'd probably run it myself, and look to franchise other ones. I'm a very ambitious person.

I like who I am and I like what I do. I like the attention, too, but sometimes I hate it. I just wish, for the sake of privacy, that I could go into a restaurant for dinner and not be bothered, not be approached for autographs. But I understand it's a part of the price I have to pay for being a sports figure. I love playing football for the New York Giants, and although I wish the money was better, I enjoy the time I share with the coaches and players. The lifestyle is good, and I have not become complacent about it. There are a lot of things I'd like to get done before my career is over, and most of them are financially motivated.

See, I know what I'd be doing if it wasn't for football, if not for this special opportunity I have received. I'd be using my hands, my body, trolling or crabbing in Louisiana. I think I would have tried to get myself through college, or at least into college, because I know that people don't really get anywhere these days without an education, especially minorities. But my family could never have sent me through school without a scholarship. There just wasn't that kind of money. In fact, both my mother and father dropped out of high school. I was the first one in my family to ever go to college. Now I'm helping my brothers and sisters do it. It's something I always felt was an obligation.

I guess you could say I am almost the sole support of my parents. Two years ago their house burned to the ground, a fire started by the spontaneous combustion of newspapers stacked in a small downstairs room. I wanted to buy them a house, move them out of Franklin to someplace nicer, maybe even move them up here to New Jersey so that we'd all be nearer to each other. But they didn't want to leave Franklin. They had lived there all their lives; all their friends were there, most of their family. They just wouldn't leave. I'm now in the process of purchasing a new brick home for my parents. And I'm paying tuition for two of the kids now. I guess in the last two years I've probably spent $60,000 on family. Hey, I'm the oldest. I'm happy to do it.

And now that I'm married again, there's a growing list of expenses and bills that must be paid. My concern with money, over what the Giants pay me, is more than just greed. Aside from my obligations, there's also my pride. I know what other players earn, I know how good they are, how well they play; then I consider my contract, how well I have played, and then I compare what I'm worth to what I earn.

The bottom line is that I'm bitter about my contract dealings with the Giants. Right now I don't think there is a lot I can do about it, but I'll say this: I'm going to play hard and play well and when my contract comes due for renegotiation, I am going to get what's fair. We negotiated during the tail end of the 1985 season, and it was such a painful experience that I felt my confidence had been seriously threatened. I was worried about whether or not I still had the same killer instinct. I was destroyed mentally by the way the Giants had handled my financial situation. They didn't seem to appreciate what I had done, how I had played, the personal sacrifices I had made, and it was—well, it was the first time I had attempted a renegotiation, so maybe I just didn't know what to expect. But it taught me something really important: This is a business, a big business, and if you don't take care of yourself, nobody else is going to give you a break. I guess I needed to learn that, and man, I really did. As for that one-day walkout in mini-camp near the end of May, I wasn't going to stay out, but I hoped it would be a way of delivering my message. I was unhappy and I wanted somebody to know it. I was making a statement by leaving, expressing my disappointment and dissatisfaction.

I was aware that my brief protest came at the start of a serious holdout of halfback Joe Morris, who turned down offers from the Giants in order to get a salary he felt was fair based on what he had accomplished the year before and what other running backs with the same accomplishments were earning. Joe did what he felt he had to do. He's one of my closest friends on the team. He's quiet, introspective. He doesn't do much in the off-season. He stays home. He and his wife, Linda, live near us. We see them socially sometimes, but man, he's a very quiet person. He's also very proud of his skills and I know he's one of the hardest working players on this team. So when he decided on a figure he felt he was worth, he wasn't going to back off. He can be very stubborn, but I guess that's what helps to make him a great running back, too.

Joe was still working with the contract he had signed as a rookie. He was supposed to play the 1986 season for $190,000, plus the bonuses that come with a spot on the Pro Bowl roster, certain yardage totals, a certain number of touchdowns and carries, playoff participation and, yes, even a Super Bowl season. Like me, he was a second-round choice, and he was scheduled to go into his option year, the extra season in the three-year contract. If agreement wasn't reached before the three-year contract ended, he would have one more year to play at no more than a ten percent raise. The purpose of this option clause, and ninety-five percent of all National Football League contracts include it, is to allow a player to become a real free agent while protecting the team against the loss of its star players without warning. It sounds fair, except for one thing. The teams in this league don't make offers to legitimate free agents. The owners won't do that to each other. So what happens is you play out the option—you can't just sit it out—and then you find out you don't have any options. Nobody is going to give you an offer. You are going to play for your original team for as long as they want you. I hope that situation gets corrected in the collective bargaining agreement between the owners and our union this year.

So Joe held out, refusing to come to camp in July because he was convinced that negotiations weren't getting anywhere. Parcells, I understand, tried to avoid a player–management confrontation, tried not to let the situation affect team morale and concentration. Bill has always been a "player's coach." He talked with Joe early in the spring. He asked him exactly what he wanted, how much it would take to make him happy, and promised he would "take the case upstairs" to the owners, Wellington and Tim Mara, and George Young. Joe agreed, so Parcells took the information upstairs and fought for the money. The Giants finally agreed. Then Joe said it wasn't enough.

Negotiations broke down and Morris finally had to decide not to report to summer camp. But even then, Parcells tried to resolve the situation. Joe insisted he wouldn't take part in any contact drills because he was afraid he'd hurt himself and lose any chance of a big contract, maybe forever. Parcells told him he wouldn't have to take part in the contact drills, but he wanted him there to attend all the meetings. He was hoping that as long as Joe stayed in good condition, which he did, he wouldn't fall behind in what the coaches were putting into the offense.

Joe agreed to that, and even though things got a little tight, he showed up, tried to ignore the media, had a little flare-up with a reporter who had called his home and spoken with his wife about the situation. That passed, but he still didn't sign. The offer went up to $500,000 a year for four years, and at that point Joe lost any chance of sympathy from the public by saying he couldn't accept it because he had a financial obligation to his family. Not many fans earn that much a year and most of their families don't suffer.

Finally, just before our first game of the season, the Monday night opener in Dallas, Joe signed for four years, $550,000 per year, plus incentive bonuses. He played, and it was the first of only two games we lost in the next nineteen. Most of the players including myself, attributed at least part of the blame for the defeat on the confusion from Joe's holdout.

You know, to a businessman, there was a lot of irony in Joe's holdout, when he finally signed. His 1,336 yards and twenty-one touchdowns the year before put him on a level with Eric Dickerson and Walter Payton, and they both earn close to a million dollars a year. The main reason the Giants held back on a bigger contract was because his previous season's performance was the first time he had ever accomplished anything like that, and they figured it might have been a one-year accident. The irony is that Joe was even better last year, gaining 1,516 yards, and if he had put together two seasons like that without negotiating after the first one, he might well have started out this season with that $1,000,000 a year contract he really wanted.

In my case, I came back after that one-day walkout, after deciding not to risk upsetting the stability of the team, and signed a new three-year agreement. The salary for the first year, this season, is $325,000. The second year it's $375,000. The third year it's $475,000. And there are incentives, bonuses for different things, that could add another hundred grand a year.

When last season started, I was worried that I didn't have the same killer instinct I had had the year before. I was almost sorry I had signed that contract. But I did it because I wanted to come back, because I didn't want to let the players down. I wanted to contribute, to be a part of the success I felt we were going to have. I didn't want to be an Al Harris or a Todd Bell, the two Bears who held out the entire season a year ago, missing the Super Bowl and some great memories. I didn't want to have to face the guys and say, "Hey, I really was there for you, but I had to do what I thought was best." You know? I didn't want that over my head. My ability as a player makes the Giants stronger. Without me at right end, I felt the team would have been weaker, and I didn't want that to happen.

So I took what was offered to me. I probably could have gotten significantly more. I thought I was worth more, but I guess my value to them as a player has yet to be shown. This contract runs through 1989, but there is a very strong possibility that I will renegotiate early. I'm not sure they'll be willing. Through a handshake and a verbal commitment with George Young I'm sure we'll be able to get something accomplished, not this season but right after that. If I'm selected to the All-Pro team again, I think they'll agree to change things. I think I'll be happy enough if they improve a few of the incentives, I can make a few extra bucks. That would bring it up to close to $500,000. I'm not where I want to be, but I haven't been in the league that long, either. So for now, I'm comfortable.

You know, it always gets back to the money. The opportunities waiting for a professional athlete who has experienced success are beyond the imaginings of most "civilians." I'm talking guys twenty-one, twenty-two years old who are jumping into million-dollar income brackets because of their ability to play a little boy's game.

Unfortunately, that's where some guys run into problems. Too much money, not enough experience, too many sharp people out there, guys looking to take advantage—it isn't all sunshine the way most people think.

For instance, I make a lot of money. But once I get through the taxes, the expenses of running different business ventures, the fees and all the rest, I won't say there isn't much left, but it sure isn't as much as I started out with. That's why I need a financial advisor like Ken Wirth. We talk every day, every day all year, just so I'll be sure of what's going on with the money and my life.

I first met Ken at a business dinner I set up at a basketball game at the Meadowlands, where I worked for two off-seasons in the public relations department of the New Jersey Sports Authority. At the time my agent and my accountant both were from D.C., things weren't going well and I didn't particularly like the guy. It was time to make a change. I just didn't like what was going on, didn't like him being there and me being here, and figured if I was involved with a guy in the New York area, I'd get more done.

Ken and I courted each other for a couple of months, and finally got things together. Ken has helped me get involved with charities, and he's helped me make some moves financially that have proved to be beneficial. I'm very pleased. Ken is one of my absolute best friends, and that's just as important to me as the investments and the money. Ken has only two professional athletes on his list, me and a teammate of mine from LSU, Lance Smith of the St. Louis Cardinals. All his other accounts are big-money people. I've met a lot of good people through Ken. My first agent didn't know money. Oh, he knew about contracts, but he didn't know money. We had some problems, some things he thought I should do that I didn't agree with. I made a few mistakes, lost some money, but I came out of it wiser. Ken started me out right from the start, making the money, saving it, helping me find the right way to handle profits. He has set me up so that I'm basically okay for the rest of my life and that's a great feeling, because I can come out of the game more mature, more aware of the business field and more financially secure than before. We weren't poor when I grew up, but we were definitely lower middle-class. I had some money in my pocket, but I had to work for everything I had.

Working was a way of life in Franklin for everyone, and the younger the better. When I was thirteen my father used to wonder where I was after school. He'd think, "Where is this kid, it's seven, eight o'clock at night." I would go to football practice, change clothes and go to work for a construction company where they'd process lye into soap. It was dangerous, sure, but I wanted the money. I was making seven dollars an hour, and that's a lot of money for a kid. At fifteen I lied about my age and worked for a gas company, digging manholes, putting down pipe for gas feeders. At sixteen I worked inside a carbon plant, where they made rubber bands, tires, and I still managed to keep my grades up.

Actually, I began to work at the age of ten, and for the next three years I cut sugar cane in the morning. I'd get up at five-thirty, cut until seven, seven-fifteen, and get four, five dollars an hour. There were white people there, too. We all needed the money.

Just like having money is a great equalizer, so is not having it. We didn't care who was black and who was white. We just worked because we needed money. I guess you might say I'm still doing that. My father once said that people say money is the root of all evil. That's not so true. It's the lack of money that's the root of evil. When you have no money to eat, you'll do just about anything.

CHAPTER 4

THAT SUPER SEASON— PART I

"After we lost the first game to the Cowboys, the rest of the season could have gone to hell."

It must have come as a great surprise to those fans who had been rooting for the Giants for years that before the 1986 season even started we suddenly were the consensus favorites to win at least the NFC Eastern championship. It was enough to freak out even the most logical minds. Here was a team that hadn't won a division title since the league began using the six-division alignment in 1970, a team that hadn't won a championship of any kind since 1963, a team that had put together some of the worst seasons with some of the most laughable excuses for pro football players in the history of the game. The Giants? Champions? No way. Even the most loyal were sure we'd find a way to screw things up.

How many times had long-suffering fans witnessed defeats that were absolutely ridiculous? Who could forget The Fumble?* Even I remember that, and I wasn't even

---

*On November 19, 1978, the Giants were playing the Philadelphia Eagles. With 31 seconds to play, the Giants held a 17–12 lead. The Eagles had no timeouts remaining. All the Giants needed to do was have quarterback Joe Pisarcik fall on the ball, and by the time he got up the clock would

in college yet when that happened. And all those last-minute losses to the Dallas Cowboys? And now the experts were saying that we were good enough to finish ahead of not only the Cowboys, who always found a way to beat us, but the Washington Redskins, too. Maybe those fans still believed in the tooth fairy, right?

Bullshit. I felt we could be champions all along, win the whole damned thing. I had started to see it the year before. We had played strong, were discovering what our younger guys could do and, more important, they were beginning to realize what they were capable of doing. The coaching staff was intact, and we were getting to know them better just as they had gotten to know us. But most important of all, we saw how well we were able to play against the good teams. We had a good season. We almost won it in 1985. We lost only six games, by a total of only 20 points. We had a one-point defeat against Dallas; we lost to Cleveland by two points; to Washington by two points; to Green Bay by three. That 10–6 record should have been 13–3, maybe even better.

After we kicked ass against San Francisco in the wild-card playoff game, we went to Chicago. And most of the Giants, including me, thought that was the turning point for what we did last year. We played on January 5 in terrible wintry conditions in Chicago's Soldier Field. They told us the wind was gusting at fifty miles an hour, that the wind-chill factor was well below zero. The Bears won the game, 21–0, and went on to win the Super Bowl XX. We knew we were just as good. So did they. Their head coach, Mike Ditka, said the Giants were the best team they had played, the toughest team all season and in the

---

have run out. But offensive coordinator Bob Gibson called instead for a play, the now infamous Pro Up 65. The snap from center Jim Clack was late. Pisarcik had to rush because fullback Larry Csonka, the intended ball carrier, was cruising past him. He never really had a handle on the ball and

playoffs, and that we had scared him the most going into the playoffs. He knew about our defense, knew it was as good as theirs was, and you know, some people even then thought we were better than their "46" scheme. Once they got past us, the Bears knew they weren't going to have much trouble. But to tell the truth, I don't think he was all that confident of getting past us. I know he'll never admit that. Why should he?

Even though it was 21–0 we played much better than that—at least the defense played very well. It's sad that we had enough chances to score against their great defense but we didn't because our own mistakes stopped us. Hey, one of their touchdowns came when Sean Landeta missed a punt and one of their guys (Shawn Gayle) took it in for a five-yard score. Now when's the last time you saw a punter miss the damned ball?

Flying back from Chicago, we felt that although the season had ended, we would be coming back smarter and tougher and better. We saw how close we were to the Bears, how if maybe we had only believed it stronger, played a little meaner, we could have won. And you better believe that we were aware of the Bears' easy run to the Super Bowl from there. Who'd they have to beat? The Los Angeles Rams in the NFC championship game? The New England Patriots? Shit, we knew they'd kick those teams all over the field. We were the only team that could have beaten them, and we screwed up. We also knew that we were going to start out from the beginning of the season and just kick ass all year.

Things started to work against us that summer, though, not that it surprised anyone. That was just part of the history of this franchise. When things were bad, they

---

when he turned to lateral it, he got only Csonka's hip. The football bounced once, and then into the arms of Philadelphia defender Herman Edwards, who scampered 26 yards for, impossibly, the game-winning touchdown.

were really bad. When things started to look good, something happened. First it was Joe Morris holding out, a bitter confrontation involving the only productive running back on the team, his agent, head coach Bill Parcells, assistant general manager Harry Hulmes and general manager George Young. The players talked about Little Joe and his financial demands. They were a little confused when he rejected $500,000 a year because he was concerned with his family's income. They tried to guess how well the replacements, like Lee Rouson and Tony Galbreath, would do. Lee was young and still learning; Tony was older and more of a pass-receiving specialist. We just didn't know how either would do if they were forced to start on an offense that had gotten used to heavy production from its running game.

Then George Adams, the number-one draft choice the year before, got hurt. As a rookie, George had looked really good as a reserve, showing us and the coaches that he was a strong runner. He had terrific potential as a receiver coming out of the backfield and was a powerful blocking back. He had gained almost 500 yards rushing, almost 400 more as a receiver, and he was going to be a great addition to our offense the next season.

At first it looked like a minor muscle pull, which is what coach Parcells told the media. Nobody thought it was anything more important than a distraction kind of thing, and since it happened during the first week of work in summer camp, nobody really thought much about it. There are guys standing on the sidelines almost every day during training camp, with little pulls and sprains. Baby stuff, nothing to worry about. Parcells said George would be back by the end of the week.

But the next week came and went and George still didn't come back. Coach Parcells still felt there was no reason for concern, that maybe it was a hamstring but not serious. Another week passed. And another. Now even the sleepiest of the reporters around the camp scene realized something serious had happened to George Adams, and that it might be a major problem, not only because George was the best replacement we had for unhappy Joe Morris but also because he had been officially moved to fullback. So that even when Joe returned, we might not see a lot of Adams in the backfield. Maurice Carthon, who doesn't carry the ball more than a few times during a game, is absolutely, with no doubt, the best blocking fullback in the National Football League today.

You know, I'm not sure Joe would have been thrilled at the idea of sharing much playing time with George Adams, because Joe likes to get as many carries as he can. As it turned out he didn't have to worry, because during practice sessions Adams just kept trotting up and down the sidelines. He didn't play in the preseason games, either. Finally Parcells informed the media what the problem was: X-rays had shown that there was a chipped pelvic bone, a difficult injury to get over because it isn't easy to fix. It just takes time. But Bill said that to write off Adams for the season would be a serious mistake, because he fully expected George to be back.

Unfortunately, he never returned—not for the season, not for the playoffs, not for the Super Bowl. Speculation was that it might have been a career-threatening injury.

So Morris was out of camp, arguing with the coaches and the sportswriters. Adams had his mysterious injury, which turned into a day-to-day thing that never got resolved, and although the Giants were hoping to take advantage of all that potential he had shown, he wasn't able to practice or play. There really wasn't anybody as talented to step in and make up not only for his loss but also for the fact that Joe still hadn't rejoined the team.

Add to all of that the lingering doubts concerning Lawrence Taylor, who had checked himself into a substance-abuse clinic. Even though everyone from team president Wellington Mara to the assistant trainers kept telling everybody that L. T. was going to be all right, nobody really knew for sure or was really qualified to make that kind of statement. Nobody ever is.

We also had the pressure of everybody picking us to win the division, the conference championship, even the Super Bowl. It wasn't a relaxing summer camp, that's for sure. With all the confusion and doubt, we ended summer camp and flew off to play Dallas in the season opener. That game was even more pressurized because it was the kickoff game of ABC's *Monday Night Football*, a nationally televised prime-time game with those damned "America's Team" Cowboys, who had just signed running back Herschel Walker from the dead United States Football League.

It's ironic: Herschel had played three seasons in Giants Stadium for the New Jersey Generals, and the Giants took a lot of criticism when Dallas signed him. After all, he's a great runner. He's 6–2, 230 pounds, he can get to be a superstar in our league. Hell, he has been a superstar since college, and then in the USFL, where he was the only great player they really had, except for quarterback Jim Kelly, who's with Buffalo now. Most of the writers who travel with us had scalded the Giants for not being willing to take a chance and draft the two-time All-America and Heisman Trophy winner.

I know Walker a little, and he's a really nice guy, but I wish we had played Georgia when I was at LSU, so I would have had some idea of what it's like to be in a game with him. Herschel had left school early to take the Generals' millions, and he wasn't eligible under NFL rules to be drafted until his college football eligibility expired. Since he had a long-term contract with Donald Trump, the real estate billionaire from Manhattan who owned the Generals and was hoping guys like Herschel and Doug Flutie would get him a franchise in the NFL, nobody seemed to think it would be smart to draft him. But the Cowboys, who always seem to take those little risks, took him in the fifth round of the 1985 draft. Then in July the USFL lost its big antitrust case against the NFL, and since it really needed to win in order to stay in business, it had no choice and disbanded. So Herschel Walker became a Dallas Cowboy early in August, and a month later, after lots of publicity he lined up to play against the New York Giants in the NFL season opener.

You could almost feel the electricity crackling through the air when Herschel made his first appearance on the field in that silver-and-blue Cowboy uniform, and it seemed almost destiny that he'd be the one to score the winning touchdown when they staged a last-minute rally to beat us, 31–28. It was a game where all the missed opportunities belonged to the Giants.

It was really depressing. Herschel scored on a designed draw play from our ten-yard line with 1:16 left in the game, and I was the outside rusher. They ran a trap play. I went on the "take" on the guy, to try to get outside him, but all I could do was try to kick the play and make it go outside, where hopefully Lawrence would have been able to make the play. I took a lot of grief. The coaches blamed me, but I won't admit that that was solely my fault. It's an eleven-man defense, and it was a play that should have been stopped. The inside linebacker should have made the stop. I tried to turn the ball carrier outside, and he stepped up inside. I didn't get sealed off, because I dove and tried to do it, but I just hit the ground. It was a lousy play on my part and by everybody else on the defense, but it was also an excellent play by Dallas. Everybody was thinking pass. They were in a shotgun formation, which reinforced the idea that it was going to be a pass. It was third down, and even if we had stopped it, I think it still might have worked on fourth down. It might have been even better to try it in a fourth-down situation, you know? People forget that Dallas made a great call, a great decision.

So Herschel took the ball and slanted to his left, in my direction, and I had started to take a fake to my right but then came back. I think I was in position to make the stop—maybe a foot or two too wide—but I got blocked. It might have been my responsibility to close down and stop him, but I just didn't get there in time. Was it my fault? I don't know. Maybe. But we lost, and because I thought we played a pretty good football game, it was even more devastating. The defense got prodded in the papers as the focal point of the defeat. But the defensive line played well, stopped the run pretty good. What we didn't do was play well together. We gave up too many long plays, too many long passes. We didn't hit people, we just were there. It just wasn't everybody's best game.

It was the third straight time we had lost to the Cowboys. Both games the season before had been close and tightly fought, but had resulted in frustrating defeats. There was a very real chance we could have started to doubt ourselves and let this one game lead to two or three more losses. Hey, we had San Diego and the Raiders coming up the next two weeks. We'd be asking for disaster if we started to think of ourselves in anything less than very positive terms. Just the way everything set up, I feel now that we just weren't meant to win that game. Too much was going on, too much negative stuff. But Parcells' most important job all that next week was to get us ready to play the upcoming Sunday, and we had one day less to practice, too.

See, all along I thought something was happening, something good for the Giants—that carryover attitude that started on the flight home from Chicago. But when we went to Dallas—I don't know—we were thinking we were so great, yet we didn't have it all together because our team was still disrupted. We had just cut our punt returner, Phil McConkey (whom we'd get back four weeks later from the Green Bay Packers, who had claimed him for nothing. We gave them a low twelfth-round draft choice). Our star running back was still not in camp. The head coach is going crazy, the assistant coaches are going crazy, the media is eating it up and Dallas is loving it. Even though they had a player out (cornerback Everson Walls), they didn't care if he was there or not. They see the Giants destroying themselves, they know we weren't going to be all together as a football team.

What we did with that loss, what Parcells did, was work from it, use it as a motivational crutch to get us moving in the right direction. He said, "Hey, guys, you've got a great football team here, but if you don't go out and play sixty minutes, play as a football team, just start hitting people and stop thinking of yourselves as a bunch of talented individuals, you're not going to get anything accomplished." Parcells made it work.

We were playing the Chargers the next Sunday, and they had just scored fifty points against the Miami Dolphins. He told the defense that if we thought it was going to be easy, forget it, because they have a quarterback named Dan Fouts, "who's going to throw 500 yards against you if you're not careful, and a running back, Gary Anderson, who's gonna run for 200 yards, and you're gonna wind up walking around with one thumb in your mouth and the other up your ass. So you better get down to business and get serious, because this ain't gonna get any easier."

And he was right. It never did. I think what Bill Parcells did right then, after our first game of the season, made us champions and made him Coach of the Year. I never saw a coach work harder to keep us up, yet be able to knock us down and make us see just how cocky we had become. We needed that game in Dallas; it was like a slap in the face with a cold towel. And Bill Parcells did for us what we wouldn't have been able to do for ourselves.

CHAPTER 5

THAT SUPER SEASON— PART II

"The team was at a low point after the opener. We were embarrassed, but still, we were a great football team."

Sometimes I think sportswriters and sports fans get too caught up with the history and tradition of a team. For instance, the New York Yankees wearing their pinstripes are always remembered for being a great baseball team. Whether they are great, good or even lousy these days doesn't really count. They are the New York Yankees wearing their pinstripes, so they must be great. The same thing is true about the Green Bay Packers. Even if right now they may be one of the worst teams in the National Football League, even if players don't really want to have to live in that boring little town, even if there is too much idle time and not enough to do, it doesn't seem to matter. All people have to do is just look at those green-and-gold uniforms and helmets, and instantly the only thing they remember is the glory days of the Sixties—Vince Lombardi and all those great players like Willie Davis, Ray Nitschke, Dave Robinson, Bart Starr and Paul Hornung—when the Packers used to win every year, and with arrogance.

My dad is like that—big on legends. I had him up here last winter after the Super Bowl. I was getting an award from the Leukemia Society at the New York Athletic Club. We're in the banquet room and he's sitting across from Dick Lynch, who does the Giants' games on the radio now but who used to be one of the league's best cornerbacks when he played on those great Giant teams. My dad was just speechless. I could see in his eyes how excited he was, and he finally says to Dick, "I remember you from a long time ago, and now here you are, smoking that big cigar and raising hell and cussing and looking just like I knew you would. You take care of my boy, Mr. Lynch. This is just like being in that television show, *Where Are They Now?*"

My point is this: Most people will sit back real sure of themselves and tell you, for instance, that Dan Fouts is the most dangerous passer in the history of the NFL, maybe better than Dan Marino in Miami, and that Fouts can win games by himself, regardless of whether he has enough blockers or receivers or what. Fouts is a legend, they tell me, and his team, the San Diego Chargers, is a fine-tuned offensive machine that is just about impossible to stop.

Hey, give me a break. The Chargers are a pretty good team, but I'll take our defense any day to hold them down. Once you make sure you approach them with the respect Fouts deserves, the rest is going to be, well, not easy, but not all that tough, not if you've done your job right.

So in our home opener six days after the Dallas game, the San Diego Chargers came to town, and we just undressed them. I mean, we beat them the way we can beat a team when we're playing very well, and I know our fans were delighted with that. But because San Diego was dangerous and we had lost our first game, we were up for this one. We had to win, and we did.

It was just the first of what would be an amazing ten straight wins at home. Nobody ever would have believed that it could happen. Hell, we wouldn't have believed it, either, if somebody had predicted it. At that point nobody on this team would even have had the imagination to be that optimistic. We were just involved in trying to beat San Diego so we'd have some steam in our engine the next Sunday when we headed for Los Angeles, where the Raiders were waiting. And no matter what we did with San Diego, nobody thought there was any way we could beat the Raiders.

After losing the opener to the Cowboys, Parcells figured (and he was right) that the team was at a low point. We had lost a tough game, a close game, because of our own mistakes. He was afraid we'd begin to dwell on it, to figure we were jinxed in close games, that we'd find a way not to win but to lose. We had been embarrassed, no doubt about it. Some of the writers had ridiculed the defense because we had allowed that last-minute touchdown by the Cowboys. We were down, and we were going to be playing a dangerous team, the Chargers. People expected us to lose, thought our season was over almost before it had started because of that one defeat to the Cowboys.

So what Parcells did was use a lot of psychology. He kept us at a low point, but kept telling us we were a great team, too. He kept telling us how badly we had played, how many mistakes we had made, although we knew we hadn't been that bad. I think by the end of the week we were angrier at him than we were at the Cowboys for winning and that's probably how he wanted us to react.

We won it, 20–7. The fans thought it was easy. The media, too. And maybe it looked that way, but it wasn't. If we hadn't pressured Dan Fouts and kept him from playing well, and if we hadn't kept Gary Anderson down to almost nothing, which was ten yards rushing and 45 as a receiver, it would have been a long day for us. We turned Fouts into just another quarterback with our defense, especially since we started to drop the linebackers deeper into the passing planes, sent defensive backs deeper to protect the end zones and demanded that the linemen provide constant pressure on Fouts. He only completed 19 of 43 passes that day, and he was hurried into five interceptions.

It's tough for me to play a guy like that. I'm always thinking about sacks, and sometimes Lamar Leachman has to calm me down and tell me to just get a lot of good hits, to make those offensive linemen tired and sore.

Dan is what I call a street player. He must have grown up with a lot of black kids because he's a gutsy quarterback, tough as a crowbar. He'll talk to you and you'll make him do something wrong and he'll still talk to you. It reminds me of when I was growing up and playing basketball in the recreational facilities back home, in Franklin. A lot of kids, if you beat them or blocked a shot, would always come back with a remark. It's fun to play against a guy like that because he makes you more competitive; you have something to prove to him. It goes along with the camaraderie of the game. After it's over, you still like the guy and you talk to him walking off the field. But while the game is being played you really want to put it to him. I like an opponent, but I like him even better when I beat him. After the game Dan smiled and told me he was throwing the ball away, that is, throwing it quickly, because he didn't want me or Lawrence to hit him.

With a passer like Fouts, you let him throw, but only if you keep pressure on him. Let him make the mistakes, let him throw it to your guys. Our defensive front and our linebackers are good enough to make up for mistakes in the secondary. That's not to say that our guys make many mistakes, but it shows how well-rounded we are as a defensive unit. Our defensive front three—Martin, Burt and myself—make up a pretty good front. I think we've finally started to prove that. What we do together helps to make up for a lot of errors. Banks and L. T. are the two top linebackers in the league. And me? Well, it's a funny thing. I hate to put myself up as better than anyone, but I guess I'm up there with the best of the defensive ends.

So we evened up our record, escaped a dangerous opponent and came through emotionally helped by the one-sided score. They had gained only 41 yards rushing, 262 yards in all, and our defense had seen to it that they'd had the ball only one-third the time of possession our offense had it. Yeah, I guess we did beat them pretty good. We played very well.

Now we had to get ready for the big, bad, arrogant Raiders, a team with some of the most outstanding players in the league: halfback Marcus Allen, defensive end Howie Long, cornerbacks Mike Haynes and Lester Hayes and tight end Todd Christensen. The Raiders have always prided themselves on physical intimidation, and they have a reputation as late-hitting cheap-shot artists. The Raiders had lost their first two games of the season, both on the road, and they were returning home to the Los Angeles Coliseum desperate for that first victory.

Maybe the Raiders were too confident. Maybe they believed all the sportswriters. Players are just as gullible as the public. So maybe all that the Raiders knew about the Giants was our recent history as a team that fumbled and bumbled and found ways to lose, a team that should be easy to beat. I guess they saw us as a springboard for getting back in the groove and ending their losing streak. In fact, Lester Hayes, a veteran who should have known better, was outspokenly contemptuous of the Giants. He showed us no respect at all, and said, "There is no way the Raiders are going to lose their first three games of the season, especially not at home, and especially not against the New York Giants."

I remember having a little trouble believing Lester would say that, and I still smile when I think about it. I guess they don't get much current news out there on the West Coast.

During that week, one of the things we talked about was how to avoid playing the way we did against Dallas. We needed to be reminded of that. We knew that as a defensive football team we had to take the game to the Raiders, had to hit Marcus Allen, had to force the quarterback to make mistakes. And we had to give our offense excellent field position so they wouldn't have to throw the ball on every down.

We were in a mean mood when we got to L.A. When the game started we took the field and just began chopping down anything that moved. Marcus Allen had to leave early in the third quarter after a violent collision at the sideline with cornerback Elvis Patterson. Early in the game we had some problems because of mental mistakes, but we settled down at halftime and came back to play an excellent game. It was also the best game I had played all season.

Our domination of the Raiders proved that we were tougher and stronger than any other defense in the league, even that of the Bears. What was even better was how we achieved the win: Giants coming back from a 6–0 halftime score, holding the Raiders to just one more field goal in the second half, scoring two touchdowns on passes from Phil Simms to Lionel Manuel and then squashing the Raiders' late rallies.

We played better in that second half, especially late in the game, than at any other time all season. It was the first time we had come back to win a game. I'll say this: That Dallas game turned out to be a good lesson. We learned a lot, and I don't think we forgot it the rest of the year. Somebody said the Raiders were impressed. They even admitted that they had been physically dominated. I remember reading what quarterback Jim Plunkett said: "It wasn't a blowout, but the Giants just did everything they had to do each time a big situation came up, especially on defense. Yes, sir, that's the best defense we've seen. I'm not sure but that it won't be the best defense we'll play all year."

I agreed with him. Even though the score was only 14–9, we knew we had done a major job on defense, shutting down a dangerous and talented team. Even Parcells, usually so guarded and cautious, finally smiled a little in front of us. He told us that was the best defensive game we'd played in some time, but that he couldn't be really happy with a 2–1 start because we never should have lost the one in Dallas. I felt the same way. I'll never concede the Cowboys were the better team that night.

Not only had we pulled our record to 2–1 and had a mini-winning streak in hand, but we had also been able to restore our pride. It was a totally different team that prepared for the second home game, the fourth game of the season, against the New Orleans Saints, a team that had never won a championship, had never even finished a season with a winning record.

As things turned out, the game could have been a damned disaster. At least it started that way. Three minutes into the first quarter the Saints shocked us with a 63-yard touchdown pass from quarterback David Wilson to wide receiver Eric Martin (once my teammate at LSU). Martin beat free safety Terry Kinard on a sideline pattern, broke a tackle by strong safety Kenny Hill and flew the final 40 yards untouched.

The Saints went on to build a 14-point lead on their next series, a touchdown drive set up by an interception and helped by a pass-interference call on Kinard. It was a bad penalty at the time because it had been third-and-13 and the pass had fallen harmlessly incomplete. So with more than three minutes still to play in the first quarter, we were down by two touchdowns. Then another damned interception right near the end of the quarter set up a Saints field goal, and all of a sudden we were staring at a 17–0 problem.

For the most part, and I think I'm trying to find some kind of reason for such an unbelievable situation, I don't think we were motivated at the beginning of the game. I know, saying you're not motivated sounds stupid. But to tell the truth, we had always thought of New Orleans as a laid-back team. Of course, we should have known better than to make such a dangerous assumption. Maybe the Raiders had been guilty of the same thing. But we had played the Saints the year before and didn't really exert ourselves, and we had won. So we really didn't go into the game convinced we had to play hard to beat them.

Now we had a big problem, and luckily we were able to wake up. Shutting out the Saints in the second half, we came back from the halftime lead they had built up and salvaged the game, 20–17. We didn't play well as a team. We didn't do everything it takes to win a game. We were lucky. We won it even if maybe we didn't deserve it.

But there was a kind of revelation during the game. For the first time that season I could sense that here was a team that didn't think they could win, didn't think they could hold us back. They were resigned to losing—just the way those old Giants teams used to be: just waiting to see how they were going to lose it.

I got my first sack of the season in that game, and it made me appreciate once again how a fraction of a second can make the difference between getting the sack and not getting it. The near-sack is one of the most frustrating parts of this game for me. I would guess that I just miss getting sixty or seventy sacks a year. Imagine how many sacks I'd have if I was a split-second faster or if the quarterback was just a fraction of a second slower.

But I guess those split seconds explain why teams spend millions of dollars on scouting—to find guys with that fraction of a second more speed. Maybe it wouldn't be sixty or seventy sacks, maybe another ten or fifteen. A whole lot of those meaningful hits would cause some fumbles, create some turnovers and some touchdowns for us.

So we closed out September with a 3–1 record, a three-game winning streak, our ego intact, our pride and confidence restored. And then, on a hot, humid day on the steaming artificial turf at Busch Memorial Stadium in St. Louis, we almost pissed it all away again. We were there to play the Cardinals, a team with a reason to be down, even more than the Saints had been at the end of our game the week before. The mistakes . . . Lord, the mistakes. We made mistakes on both sides of the line of scrimmage; we didn't go out to kill anybody, really put away St. Louis. Mind you, the Cardinals were 0–4 at that point. They had a new coach, Gene Stallings, and he was just trying to find a way to win. His team was ready to play and we weren't. They gave us a lot of problems. They shut down our running game, making it tough for us to win. Defensively we tried to make some adjustments, to make things easier for our offense, like knocking the ball loose, giving our guys good field position, at least setting up a field goal.

What was the matter with us? There we were, the New York Giants, winners of three straight, three of four, moving into position to challenge for a first-ever division championship, and facing a team that was without a doubt inferior and struggling. How could we not have been ready to play a game like that? I think it was lack of motivation, overconfidence, being too humble, giving a team too much respect, not going out there to kill them, to really put them away. For a long time people had said that the Giants cannot win consecutively, that they always rise to the occasion to beat the good teams but they cannot beat the terrible teams. We were playing a team that knew it couldn't beat us, and we had to show them they were right: They couldn't beat us, no matter how well they played. But they almost did. I think that woke us up.

In order to win, and win convincingly every week, you have to be ready to play every game, because the better your team is, the harder the other team is going to play. You can't afford to relax, because in this league, even the team that hasn't won a game has great players who can put together a perfect game and beat the best teams. Personally, I wasn't ready to play that day. Oh, I made some plays, but I wasn't ready. I think I was still brooding about why I signed a deal I didn't want and didn't like. It was on my mind a lot. I just wasn't ready to get everything done that day, and even though I played well and helped us win, stuffed the run pretty good, I wasn't ready to play.

Even so, we won by the score of 13–6. Afterwards, coach Parcells said that luck, and lots of it, was involved. He said these are the kinds of games you love to win because you can fix the things that went wrong, but you can never change the score. He said we were fortunate to get the hell out of there with a win. I agreed at least two hundred percent.

The key to any game is finding the rhythm, the feel of it, the flow, how it's happening, and why. I thought we played better in the second half, but in the first half we didn't get it together as a unit. There is no doubt that the Cardinals deserved to win it more than we did. They played harder. I went into that game not respecting offensive tackle Luis Sharpe, and he made a lot of good plays against me. But I got some things done that I wanted to, and established some respect for me in his mind. I had two sacks in the game. So did Lawrence Taylor. So did Carl Banks. No questions about it, the defense was beginning to rumble.

We flew home with the winning streak up to four, the record at 4–1, and the Philadelphia Eagles our next opponents. That's always one of the better teams for me to play against. I always seem to get a lot of sacks and tackles behind the line of scrimmage.

We were looking forward to the Eagle game. We wanted to show Buddy Ryan what kind of team we had, show him that the Giants were the team he had to beat to win the division. That was what he said the Eagles were going to do. Buddy said a lot of things. It was his way, I guess, coming from Chicago. He said he didn't see any reason why he couldn't beat the Giants both times. In fact, he said he didn't see any reason why he couldn't beat all four other teams in the division twice each.

I knew Ryan had built his defense in Chicago, the famous "46" defense that had taken the Bears through the league in 1985, losing only one game all year and then breezing in the Super Bowl. As a result, Buddy Ryan got an offer from the Eagles' owner to become their new head coach. I have always wondered, if he was such a great defensive coach, how come after eighteen years as an assistant coach, he had never been offered a head-coach job before. Nobody seems to know why, but anyway, he took the job, of course, and started shooting off his mouth right away.

He said that he knew all he needed to know about the Giants. He knew what Joe Morris could do, and Phil Simms, and the defense. And how did he know this? He remembered what the score was in the playoff game the year before. Weren't all those guys on the team then, too? So what should he be afraid of?

Man, I can't tell you how much that pissed me off. He should have worried about not having the Bears' players, for one thing. What's more, he didn't realize just how good the Giants had become in less than one year, and we were anxious to prove it. The opportunity to show Buddy Ryan the light of day was too good to resist. I was really ready for that game.

We beat them, 35–3.

It seemed like the Eagles were very lackadaisical that day. It was a typical Eagle team, and I didn't see what difference it made having Buddy Ryan as their coach. They just couldn't adjust to our changing tactics. No doubt, they're one of our top rivals, and it's always important that we beat them. As long as I'm a Giant, I hope we never lose to the Eagles.

Coach Parcells just smiled and shrugged his shoulders when the writers asked him about the score and whether he had intentionally run it up against Ryan. I guess it looked obvious. Late in the game he went with a fake field goal when we were already ahead by 21–3. Our backup quarterback, Jeff Rutledge, threw a 13-yard touchdown pass to Harry Carson. All Bill said was, it was a chance for our offense to get some points. We had been playing a lot of close games, so why not let them build their confidence?

Anyway, it was pretty obvious that Ryan didn't respect us much, didn't respect the players, thought Taylor and I were overrated, thought the whole football team was overrated, our coaching staff, too. He said he didn't feel the Giants were a team to contend with in the East. It's funny, but if St. Louis had won just a couple more games, Buddy Ryan would have been at the bottom of the pile, you know? In last place. Well, maybe next year.

After the season was over, somebody said Ryan had manufactured those statements to get his team aroused, knowing that the Eagles weren't really competitive, hoping this would be one way to put pressure on them to play better, perhaps to inspire them to reach heights they were not capable of reaching. There's all sorts of ways to do it, but knocking another team isn't the best way to motivate your own. The best way to motivate a team is to show them films, show them things they've done well, things they can do, basic fundamentals that got them where they are.

Did I play well? Oh, yeah, I have to play well against them. I always do. They cut the guy I played against, somebody named Tom Jelesky. I was going through him almost anytime I wanted. We sacked the quarterbacks six times; Lawrence had four, and I helped open lanes for some of those. We held their running game to almost nothing, 59 yards, and Randall Cunningham, the second-string quarterback, had 24 of those. It was a great game, and beating them was a great feeling, especially after all those things Ryan had said.

But as much fun as beating Buddy Ryan had been, we had to forget about it. We had another tough road game to play the next Sunday in the Seattle Kingdome, a pressure-cooker where the fans are louder than anywhere else in the league and where the noise, trapped by the dome, just beats down on you so that you can't hear. It is the toughest place to play in the league, everybody says so. The fans make so much noise the linemen can't hear the quarter-back without turning their heads, and when they do they lose sight of the defensive guys. There should be some rule passed to stop the fans from taking that kind of unfair advantage. It just isn't right.

We couldn't use our shotgun formation because that put Phil Simms too far away from the line, and nobody could hear him.

We got beat, 17–12. Looking back, it was memorable for only one reason: It would be the last time we'd lose a game in the next three months. The defeat put us at 5–2.

I thought we played well, but we made mistakes, some of them due to the noise. We busted some assignments on defense but it's always like that; when you lose by a close margin it's always just one or two plays. I think we talked ourselves into expecting that the noise was going to be a problem. The coaches were practically paranoid about the noise. We practiced all week with loudspeakers on the field and a noise machine going on and off at various inter-vals. It was just a crazy week.

Then we got out there and the weather was gloomy. And I guess we were, too. We played well, but we made just enough mistakes to lose it. If we had played them at home, we would have won, because the noise wouldn't have been a factor. But hell, if we had played all sixteen games in Giants Stadium, I think we probably would have won them all.

The way those Seattle fans took advantage of the noise got us angry. We felt like we cheated ourselves, letting ourselves lose a game like that. It was like we had left something on the field. The guys looked back on that game as a landmark, saying things like: "Hey, remember that day in Seattle, when we dropped that ballgame we should have won." That was the game that carried us the rest of the season without losing.

So after Seattle we were looking straight down the barrel of a loaded shotgun. The next seven games were going to be against Washington, Dallas, Philadelphia, Minnesota, Denver, San Francisco and Washington again. You want the truth? Not even I figured we'd win them all.

CHAPTER 6

THAT SUPER SEASON— PART III

"I don't think anybody expected us to win those next seven games. Nobody. Nobody but the Giants."

Now should have been the time for us to crash, to hit the water in flames. And why not? The Giants had always done exactly that at such critical junctures for as long as even the most dedicated fans could remember. The myth: The Giants never really win anything in the long run. They just get close sometimes, and then as soon as some really together team comes along, they find a way to drop a pass in the end zone. The fans get real disappointed but, what the hell, they all come back next week and give the team a standing ovation because it was a close game and the guys tried real hard. End of myth. Despite the loss to Seattle, now was the time to show that we were on the way to becoming an outstanding team.

That Seattle defeat was tough for us to accept. Our winning streak was over, and so was our share of first place in the East. The Dallas Cowboys were coming on tough, and now they were 5–2, tied with us but with momentum on their side. The fact that we had lost to them gave them a psychological edge.

The Redskins at that moment were clearly the cream of

the crop, with a 6–1 record, including a victory over Seattle. Although that wasn't a critical edge over a division team, it could still give them a tie-breaker edge if we finished the season tied.

There they were, those damned Redskins, tough and cocky, rough and ready, coming to Giants Stadium for a nationally televised Monday night game. They were ready to show us that we didn't really belong in this thing, ready to beat us and send us home convinced that second place would be okay, that another wild-card playoff spot would be the best we could hope for.

Parcells was at his best the week before this one. He told us that the Redskins were the best team in the league, that he wasn't sure we'd be up to beating them. He told us about their experience, their size, how they played with that street-fighter mentality, how they were the toughest team to "kill" because of their ability to come back and win in the final seconds of a game. He really liked the Redskins. He had great respect for their coach, Joe Gibbs, and for how they played. I think he wanted us to be like them: tough, strong, able to stand up and take everything a team wanted to hand out and then just win.

Bill has always been impressed by the size of their linemen, on both sides of the line. Like defensive tackle Dave Butz, who's 6–7 and at least 300 pounds. Bill got a laugh from the writers when he said Butz was so big he should have his own zip code. Their guys on the offensive line seemed to give Parcells some kind of joy just looking at them. He told us that they were as good as they were big. They had bruisers like Joe Jacoby, a guy I had seen too damned much, maybe the biggest guy I've ever had to play—he's only 6–7 and weighs 315—and Russ Grimm, who at 6–4 and 290 is just as tough.

He didn't have to tell me about those two guys. I had already spent three years trying to get through them, or around them. They were the best guard–tackle pair I've had to deal with—the best in the league. I mean, they are just gigantic people, and the whole line is a good one. With a good running back like George Rogers, a smart young quarterback like Jay Schroeder and two outstanding receivers like Art Monk and Gary Clark, I knew the game was going to be a bitch for our defense. It always had been.

I've never admitted this before, but I was scared to death before that game, before the second Washington game and absolutely before our championship game. No matter who else we had to play, I figured we were tougher and that would eventually win it for us. But I'm not so sure we thought we were tougher than the Redskins. There are so many similar things about both teams that we knew what to expect and so did they. It came down to who did it better. No fancy shit, no silly plays to try and fool your opponent. Just stand there face to face, and beat the hell out of each other, big guys against big guys, great running backs against great running backs. The Redskins are always tough, and they're tough the way we are. They beat you and they hurt you. Now, how the hell were we supposed to deal with that?

The week before that game, one of the assistants on the coaching staff, offensive line coach Fred Hoaglin, told Washington-area sportswriters about the difficulties of blocking Butz. "Butz is so big his head looks like it weighs fifty pounds, looks like a damned pumpkin." The press and the other Redskins loved it, as you could imagine, and when Butz got to practice the next morning, he found his locker full of pumpkins. Chris Godfrey, our "little" right guard (he's 6–3 and 260) just about had a fit when he heard that. "No, he didn't say that about Butz, did he? He didn't get that big man angry, did he? Oh, God."

The game setting itself was unreal, and I don't think we'll ever play in that kind of situation again. It was the night of the seventh game of the World Series, that great series between the New York Mets and the Boston Red Sox. Many of the football fans showed up at Giants Stadium with miniature television sets so they could watch the series as well. Frequently during the football game, when no cheering was called for, they would suddenly yell and scream from the seats when the Mets did something good.

Even the Redskins found it weird. Schroeder, whom I got to know a little at the Pro Bowl and who seems like a really nice guy, said that one time it seemed they were cheering for him when he completed a pass, but then he remembered where he was and that no sane Giant fan would ever cheer a Redskin.

I'm not sure if the Giant fans I know would rather we beat the Redskins or the Cowboys. Maybe it's a tie, but I know they sure as hell love it when we beat Washington. I think it probably has something to do with all those games the Redskins won when George Allen was coach—twelve or thirteen in a row—and some of the things he did that made Giants fans feel so frustrated, like calling time out with nine seconds to play so he could kick a field goal when the Redskins were already ahead by three touchdowns; or stopping the game when his team was on the Giants' one-yard line so a back could get another touchdown or a first down. Hey, that would piss me off, too. I don't blame the fans, and I'm kind of sorry Allen wasn't coaching last year.

Everybody was tight, tense; we all knew it was Washington Week, Redskin Week; we knew we had to win it. Monday nights are tough, because you try to stay calm all day and you can't, there's too much going on. All the other games that week have been played, and the whole league is waiting to see what you're going to do. The whole country too.

We played ferociously. After the Seattle game nobody gave us a chance against Washington. All we knew was that it was a game we had to win, and in order to win it, we had to come out smoking early. The defensive line had to pressure the quarterback. We had to stop Rogers, who had been averaging 100 yards a game up to then. We held him to very little. Rogers gained 30 yards in 16 carries, less than two yards per rush. We were able to sack Schroeder four times, three of them by Lawrence Taylor. The defense intercepted two passes, one by cornerback Perry Williams that led to a touchdown pass from Phil Simms to wide receiver Bobby Johnson for 30 yards. The offense took control early. It was 10–3 at halftime, 20–3 near the end of the third quarter, and the stadium was rocking with the prospect of a double victory, since the Mets were beating the Red Sox. Everything was coming out right, and we were really on our way. I was even happy for the Mets. And then all that stuff Parcells had been warning us about began to happen. His predictions—the Redskins can rally at any time, from any score, and scare the shit out of you, that they can get you no matter how far ahead you are—seemed to be coming true.

Suddenly our comfortable 20–3 lead became 20–10 and then 20–17. Then about eleven minutes into the fourth quarter, their placekicker, Max Zendejas, nailed a 29-yard field goal and the score was tied at 20–20. The only cheering from the stands then was for the Mets. The Giants were starting to blow their biggest game of the season. The Redskins kept right on doing what they had been trying to do all game, and I think that's the mark of a smart, well-coached team. Being behind didn't panic them, didn't make them try all kinds of new shit that might have gotten them deeper in a hole. They just kept slugging and fighting and trying those passes, and all of a sudden it was all working. Man, that was a very gutty team that night. I don't think I've ever had more respect for a team. They were blocking really well, and even when we got through and hit Schroeder, he stood in the pocket and took the hits. And I can tell you we were really laying some wood on him.

Until the Redskins did their comeback trick, it was really a defensive night for us. We were playing hard, and I couldn't believe, good as they were, that they were going to be able to steal this game from us.

Finally, with the help of a few penalties, we put together one last drive in ten plays for 81 yards. Joe Morris gained 66 of those yards, including the winning touchdown from the 13 with 1:38 left on the clock. Joe was in top form and finished the night with 31 carries for 181 yards. And he had 59 more yards on five catches.

I also played well against the Redskins, very well. And it was especially satisfying to me that I played well against Jacoby and Grimm. Lawrence and I were finally able to do a consistent job on those two sides of beef. When I went outside, Lawrence came up the middle. When I went inside, Lawrence came from the outside. Sometimes I'd line up inside and the other tackle would come around me. Or I'd line up wide and then make an inside move. Jacoby isn't the biggest guy I've ever played—Anthony Munoz with Cincinnati is—but Jacoby is strong and very agile for a big man. But I'm a lot quicker than most defensive ends, so if he doesn't make contact with me right away, I'm going to get behind him and he's going to wind up getting beat. Jacoby's got good balance, but not good enough against a guy as big and strong as me, because I can get past him and throw him, too.

When I first came into the league, Jacoby and Grimm gave me more trouble than anybody. And now all of a sudden we're beating them, they're moaning about it, and I'm getting around and through them. It showed me just how much I had improved in three years. I was really happy about that. They were even complimenting me on the field during the game. I remember Grimm saying, "How can you be so damned fast, you're so big." And

Jacoby said, "Nice move, how the hell do you and Taylor keep working that same stunt? We know you're gonna do it and you're still getting away with it."

The five-game stretch beginning with Washington was our best. We had to prove to ourselves and to the other teams that we deserved a playoff spot, and a championship; we were as good as our record showed and not just lucky. Some people were saying we were lucky to have beaten the Redskins the week before. Bullshit. Ask them how much luck it took. Then ask them how much talent it took.

Now we were really into the stretch drive, and that victory, sweet as it was, had to be forgotten the next morning. In six days the Cowboys were coming, and we couldn't allow ourselves the luxury of savoring anything for too long. If we did, we'd start to get into that frame of mind we were in when we opened the season in Dallas, with the attitude that we were a great team and all we had to do was show up. Those damned Cowboys were going to be ready. They were still in the race, and they just wouldn't believe we could beat them. In fact, we almost never did, except in 1984, when we beat them twice. But this one coming up was a game we absolutely had to win, and not just because we needed to erase our embarrassment over that earlier fiasco.

We hadn't executed well that first game. Nobody had. The ball must have been fumbled four times by our new punt returner, rookie cornerback Mark Collins (who had replaced Phil McConkey after the Giants had waived him). Collins had so much trouble fielding punts that, despite his great speed and moves, the Giants knew they had to get McConkey back. We made too many mistakes in our running and passing game. The secondary made mistakes. The defensive line didn't keep up the pressure. That was our defense's worst game, definitely. So now we got them again and we're on a roll, and we have a vendetta going.

The second game against the Cowboys was another one of those nailbiters we perfected during the Super Bowl season. We won it, 17–14. We won because George Martin, the left defensive end, was thirty-four years old and experienced, and Dallas offensive tackle Phil Pozderak was twenty-seven and inexperienced. Still, we almost lost that game. For a while it looked almost certain that we were going to screw it up and waste a great chance. But then George took an overdose of Geritol and made a fool out of that Pozderak kid. He came up with a great game. I had played against Pozderak in the first game, since he was lined up on my side then. He's not a very good tackle, but he's gigantic, 6–9 and at least 290, and he has great long arms. That's the thing he has going for him. If I'm put one-on-one with him, I'm sure I could beat him. But that first time, I had never played him and didn't know how to play him. It was Martin's best game of the year, no doubt, and he made that kid look silly.

The Giants and the fans were celebrating their tenth anniversary in Giants Stadium. Ten years ago when the stadium opened Dallas had also been the opponent and the Cowboys won that game easily. (The most popular trivia question I've heard about the Giants is who scored the first touchdown in Giants Stadium? Well, it's kind of embarrassing when you hear the answer. Robert Newhouse did. A Dallas Cowboy, not a Giant.) The Giants were terrible that year, in the middle of a 3–11 season, and Dallas won that first-ever game, 24–14. In fact, right after a seventh loss in a row the Giants fired their head coach, the only time in Giant history that a coach didn't finish out a season.

Now things were different. We were a team on the move, a team that was going to live up to its destiny, and if it took an old man to make it happen, then George

Martin was happy to step up and have his gray hairs counted.

It happened late in the fourth quarter. The Cowboys had just scored on a 23-yard draw by halfback Tony Dorsett, capping a great 90-yard, nine-play drive with young Scott Pelluer at quarterback. He had replaced veteran Danny White, who had been knocked out for the game (and for the rest of the season) with a broken right wrist as a result of Carl Banks' sack. The Pelluer kid was sensational, and suddenly, with seven-and-a-half minutes still to go, what once was a safe 17–7 Giant lead was now a tight 17–14, just a field goal away from sudden death and a touchdown away from a defeat.

We got the ball but couldn't go anywhere and had to punt. We managed to stop Dorsett, whom we considered the Cowboys' chief weapon. But all of a sudden Pelluer, whom we didn't expect to play, was getting hot. He's more mobile than White, and he runs around to buy time. He can also take off and scramble, making him more dangerous and adding another dimension to the ways he can beat you. I'll say this about the Pelluer kid. He showed me a lot. He was under great pressure and he played with poise. He was very cool. Truthfully, I've seen Danny White get rattled more than that kid did.

Anyway, we thought the situation was safe enough, because they had to get things started from their 16-yard line. Teams just don't move that easily against us, especially when they have to pass and we know they have to pass. But suddenly the kid found the range. He threw for seven yards to running back Herschel Walker, then five to fullback Timmy Newsome for a first down. We started to pull in the secondary because he was going for the short stuff. Then he hit tight end Doug Cosbie for 20 yards and the Cowboys were in our half of the field, on our 48, at the two minute warning.

When he came back, with different defenses called,

different zone coverages and a change-up in pass rushing, Pelluer still managed to find Herschel Walker for a five-yard gain. But then he showed his inexperience. He wanted to pass, but I chased him after I had broken free of a two-man block. I got clear (yeah, there was some holding, too, but nobody ever calls that anymore, it seems) and I was all alone in the backfield, running him down. I had a clear shot, but the kid just did throw the ball away. Now, I don't want to criticize the officials, even if they do miss so many times when I'm being held, but the holding had been so flagrant that they had to do it. They called him for intentional grounding. That cost Dallas a lot because it wasn't just ten yards but loss of down too.

So it was third-and-15 at the Cowboys' 43. The clock said 1:22, and that damned kid threw a 21-yard pass to rookie wide receiver Mike Sherrard at our 36.

Then George Martin slipped into a nearby telephone booth, and after getting rid of his old man's clothes and walking stick, he stepped out of it George Martin, Superstar. He beat Pozderak so badly on the next play, an attempted pass, that the kid had no choice but to hold him. The yellow flag took away a completion to Tony Dorsett, 30 yards downfield on our six-yard line. The ball came back and then some, to our 46. Now it was first-and-20. Pelluer hit Walker for five, and then the Cowboys got a break after Lawrence Taylor was flagged for defensive holding, only a four-yard penalty but it got them a first down. Pelluer moved Dallas even closer, to our 26, and from there no worse than a field goal was guaranteed, and overtime was in the cards.

Hold on, now. George has taken another swig of Geritol, whispered a prayer to St. Arthritis, and did it again. He showed Pozderak an inside fake, crossed the kid's legs, then slipped past him to nail Pelluer with a 15-yard sack, all the way back to our 41. From there, a field goal attempt would be 58 yards long, not likely for a short-range place kicker like Rafael Septien.

It was third down now, 25 yards to go, only 33 seconds left on the play. And then Pelluer did it again, this time hitting Newsome for 30 big yards. The Cowboys were supposedly on our 11-yard line.

But hold on, bring that play back! George Martin had done it to Phil Pozderak still again, one more time in the same series, making him look silly. Old George sure played like a kid that day, and we needed him more than any of us had ever thought we would. Exactly what had George done?

He used one of the oldest tricks in the game. Just as they were ready to snap the ball, George threw his arm at Pozderak. And he flinched. He moved. That's a penalty, false start. The flag came down and the play didn't count. The ball was moved back another five yards, to the 46. We had it locked up.

When the gun finally sounded two plays later, Septien was well short with a monster 63-yard field goal attempt. If that had gone through, I would have collapsed and died right there on the field. Septien just doesn't kick that long.

There was just a sliver of difference between winning and losing that game, and that Pelluer kid really put a fright into us. I mean, he was cool, really poised. He's going to be a good one. He doesn't say a word, just goes about his business. Oh, Dorsett talks a little, but see, Tony doesn't like to get hit, kind of resents it when you do nail him, like he doesn't deserve to be treated that way. He's a moaner, you know?

So we were 7–2. The writers were making hourly trips to the record books, not only to find the ones we had broken but also to get ready for those just waiting around the corner with our next victory. Not since 1963, I learned, not since Y. A. Tittle, Frank Gifford, Andy Robustelli and

Sam Huff, had a Giant team been 7–2, and that team went on to win once more before losing. It seemed like everybody was getting excited. People in the street, in the stores, business people, truck drivers, waitresses. Everybody. It was a very exciting time to be in New York because the Jets were even better than us at 8–1, and everybody was figuring we were going to meet them in the Super Bowl. Can you imagine that, if we played the Jets in the Super Bowl? What a trip that would have been. The Jets were to run their record to a fantastic 10–1 but then stumbled, crippled by injuries to key defensive starters, and lost their last five games to barely qualify for the playoffs as a wild-card team. I'd like to say that if they hadn't gotten hurt—and remember, they lost Gastineau, Klecko, Mehl and Lyons, which is just as if we had lost Martin, Burt, L. T. and me, for instance—if they hadn't had that kind of rotten luck, I think they would have been the best team in the American Conference and would have made it to the Super Bowl, or at least gotten awfully damned close. Man, how I would have loved that. Can you imagine?

In contrast, we were healthy and just beginning to feel our strength. We went down the New Jersey Turnpike for the rematch with the Philadelphia Eagles. Buddy Ryan's Eagles, who were supposed to be motivated by the fact that we had tried to embarrass them by running up the score the first time around. It apparently fired them up, because they tried to intimidate us early—in a somewhat ugly fashion.

The incident happened in the second quarter. The first quarter had been scoreless, but then we took advantage of a partially blocked punt (by our third-string quarterback, Jeff Hostetler, of all people), took possession at the Eagles' 48 and moved in for the touchdown when Joe Morris ran the last 18 yards.

Joe was standing in the end zone, the play was over and

the touchdown signal had already been given, for God's
sake, when one of the Philadelphia cornerbacks, Evan
Cooper, grabbed Joe around the chest, spun him around
and threw him against the retaining wall behind the end
zone. Joe hit the wall with his head, and it was a very
frightening thing. He slumped to the ground, motionless.
It was suddenly very quiet in Veterans Stadium.

. The penalty flags came from all over, of course, but
unsportsmanlike conduct is only 15 yards. We wanted
Cooper's head. Joe slowly got to his feet and, after shaking
his head, trotted off. A disaster had almost taken place,
and even if it hadn't, the intent had been there. I'm still
not sure that Cooper didn't do it on purpose, or if, like he
said later, he was just so pissed that Joe had beaten him
that he didn't think. Either way, there's no place for shit
like that in the NFL, and the officials were wrong when
they didn't throw his ass right out of the game. And
maybe for a couple more after that one, too. You try to
play clean, try to enjoy playing other guys, try not to hurt
other people. But on that particular day they were trying
to hurt people. That's lousy. I asked wide receiver Mike
Quick about Cooper, and he said he was surprised, the kid
wasn't usually like that. I don't know, maybe he was just
trying to make Buddy Ryan happy.

I heard Cooper was later fined $2,500 by commissioner
Pete Rozelle after the league people watched the videotape. Big deal. That's just chump change compared to
what he could have done to Joe and his family and the
good name of the game.

The defense was sensational once again. Seven times
we sacked their quarterbacks, Ron Jaworski and Randall
Cunningham. L. T. had three of them and I had one-and-
a-half. You know, Jaworski is gone this year. The Eagles
waived him, and although I don't know if they were smart
to do that or not (that's their business and not mine) I

was very impressed with the Cunningham kid. I think he's going to be a really good quarterback if the Eagles can get him some blockers. That's still the team I always have my best games against. Harry Carson had nine solo tackles, and after we killed them with a quick 17–0 explosion, we just relaxed and won our second consecutive 17–14 game.

The record was now 8–2. "The Play" was coming next.

CHAPTER 7

THAT SUPER SEASON— THE MIRACLE PASS

"Are you kidding me? How could we ever lose again after something like that?"

First of all, I'd like it to be known that the Giants' defense is not just the best in the National Football League. It's the toughest, too. It has the toughest, meanest people. We play clean, never dirty, but we play tough. And we are very good at convincing people it isn't smart to try to intimidate the Giants. It's not gonna work.

Sure, there are other teams that boast strong, effective defenses. Some teams even seem to relish the reputation of having a dirty defense. The dirty players—guys who take cheap shots, try to hurt other guys—they're out there, all right. In my book, the Forty-Niners always take cheap shots, trying to hurt people. Some teams just hate the Giants. The Cowboys hate the Giants. I know it. I think the Giants have become the team to hate now. We try to go out and intimidate people, but we don't try to play dirty.

Not even Kenny Hill, our strong safety who seems to play with a constant chip on his shoulder. He's aggressive and determined and he makes up for a lot of things by playing hard, but dirty football is not his bag. Hey, Kenny Hill is a Yale graduate with a bachelor's degree in molecular biophysics, who takes premed courses at UCLA. He usually draws a penalty flag for unsportsmanlike conduct at least once every other game. Kenny Hill is the guy who was fined five thousand bucks for a late hit against San Francisco in the playoffs, but from what we know about the Forty-Niners, that might well have been a case of retaliation. Oh, Kenny Hill is just crazy, he just loves that intimidation factor. He used to be a Raider, and that's the whole deal with the Raiders. They preach intimidation to their players. You always see their guys getting thrown out of games. But we don't see it that way, because if you're a starter your value to us is to be in the game, not on the bench.

All of this brings to mind the game we played in the Hubert H. Humphrey Metrodome in Minneapolis on Sunday, November 16, 1986. It was our first appearance in the new, enclosed stadium, and it was our first meeting with the Minnesota Vikings since a 24–7 loss in 1976.

The game in the Metrodome was one neither team will ever forget. Never. If I ever get amnesia, that game will be the only thing I'll remember. I'll forget my name before I forget that play.

It happened with just 1:12 remaining in the game. The Vikings held a 20–19 lead, and it appeared almost certain that our newest winning streak was going to die at three, that the record was going to fall to 8–3 and that the Redskins were going to take undisputed possession of first place in the Eastern Division.

All of that was just 72 seconds away. We were on our own 48-yard line, following a nine-yard sack of quarterback Phil Simms by defensive end Doug Martin, George's younger brother. It was fourth down. And 17 yards to go. Imagine. No margin for error. No second chance. There were 62,000 fans who hadn't left yet because this had been a heart-stopping game and they wanted to rise at the gun and savor the upset. The Vikings were on their way to a strong season, and they were starting to build up their hopes for a playoff spot.

So it was fourth-and-17 on an unfamiliar field, and in a situation like that, as Phil Simms described it, "seventeen yards looks about as long as three football fields." The noise level was almost as intimidating as it had been in Seattle—where we had lost our last game a month earlier. The Viking defense was confident and why not? What could the Giants possibly do besides throw the ball? They knew that. They were playing deep, willing to give up a short pass, knowing that it was fourth down. They knew that as soon as the play failed to come up with the yardage we had to have, their offense would take over, their quarterback would fall on the ball and they would watch the clock eat up the final seconds. Right?

Simms, who would later say it was one of the easiest passes he had ever thrown, took the snap, dropped back into a tightly formed pocket of protection ("I remember," said offensive tackle Brad Benson, "thinking that if anybody tried to get through to him on that play I would give up my life to stop him") and began looking downfield. Phil has said he was looking for Phil McConkey first, but that he couldn't find him. Then he scanned the middle of the field for tight end Mark Bavaro. He was covered. So he went to Bobby.

Bobby Johnson, our other wide receiver, had calmly run down the right sideline, straight as an arrow. By design. He said later that he'd decided to run it like a deep route, like he was going for the touchdown. Then he suddenly pulled up. "I had seen the yard marker as I ran by, so I knew if I caught the ball we'd have the first down," he said.

When Bobby jammed on the brakes, the cornerback Issiac Holt was doomed—killed by his own momentum as he kept going downfield. Simms threw a perfect square-out that Johnson caught on his tiptoes just at the sideline. "It was a perfect pass," Bobby told the writers later, "not too hard, not thrown too slow. I knew we had the first down. I also knew if I dropped that one I would have to walk home from Minneapolis."

I smiled when somebody told me what Johnson said, because I *know* we wouldn't have let him get on the plane. But he didn't drop it. Instead, he made a perfect two-handed grab. He clutched that ball to his chest, and set the Giants' bench on fire.

I never heard a team on the sidelines come alive so quick, and so loud, from just one play. Everybody was yelling and screaming. It was like nobody could believe what had just happened. But the funniest thing, the thing I will always remember, was Lamar Leachman, who was standing on the bench—I always start to laugh before I can finish this story. He was standing up there to see the play, and when Phil threw the ball to B. J., Lamar starts running "with him" on the bench. And just when it looks like Bobby's gonna catch the ball, a second before he actually does catch it, Lamar runs out of bench, falls flat on his face from a running start, jumps up and yells, "What happened? What happened?" I told him that Bobby Johnson just made the biggest, best and most important catch of his whole damned career and that Lamar missed it because he fell on his face. He had to look at the scoreboard to make sure it really was first down and I wasn't just fooling him.

We had known it was going to take a miracle to win that game, and what we got was a miracle. The Vikings were finished and they knew it. You could see their players on the field just sag. The pass put us on the 30-yard line. The clock showed 1:06 remaining, and on the next play Doug Martin, who had almost been the hero, jumped offside, moving the ball to the 25. After that Joe Morris ran a slant through the right guard/right tackle hole for eight yards; then hit right guard again for two.

Now there were just 22 seconds to go. Morris positioned the ball for place kicker Raul Allegre's upcoming field goal attempt by diving into the middle of the line for no gain, centering the ball for the kick and lining up a perfect head-on shot from 33 yards out. The snap was perfect, and with 12 seconds left, on third down—not fourth—the ball sailed perfectly through the uprights. (We had decided to kick on third down just in case something happened—a fumble or whatever—so we could recover and kick again. That's just good sense.) After the game, for the first time all season, even Parcells couldn't keep us from celebrating. It was the loudest locker room of the year. McConkey challenged the sportswriters, daring someone to say the Giants don't have any good receivers. That had been bothering him all season and why not? He's a receiver, isn't he? And nobody ever put more effort into playing the game. So he was screaming, all red in the face, and the players were yelling and Parcells was smiling. It was a very strange, very happy locker room. It had been a miraculous win.

Coach Parcells finally reacted to some midseason criticism of Simms from some of the writers. He scolded them a little, saying that anybody who thinks Phil Simms can't play quarterback should be covering another sport. And he's right. Phil had one of the greatest seasons a quarterback has ever had. But some of the writers who cover the Giants are just never going to be happy.

We all came away from the victory thrilled, of course, some of us thinking that maybe it had made up a little for the Seattle game. We also came away with a new, deeper respect for that Minnesota squad. The Vikings were a really good team that day. Their defense rolled around, kept pressure on Phil, intercepted passes and shut down our running game. It took five field goals to beat them, and we usually have better luck on offense, usually scoring a few touchdowns when we have to have them. I would say that the Vikings were the best team we played all season, at least on that day. And the win was more dramatic because of the down and distance, and the time left. Lucky? Sure, why not? Great teams can be lucky, too. We had a string of games going, had won four in a row—our longest streak of the season—and we wanted five.

The guys were chanting, "Two days off, two days off," which we got every time we won a game. It meant we didn't have to come in for practice or meetings on Monday or Tuesday—normally work days—but only if we won.

Now it was Denver coming up at home, and we knew the Jets had beaten them badly earlier in the season by putting pressure on their quarterback, John Elway, early in the game. The game—a rare meeting, the first since 1980—was starting to look like a possible Super Bowl preview simply by the process of elimination. The injury-ridden Jets, who at one time had a 10–1 record, had fallen badly. Besides Gastineau, Klecko and Mehl, other players kept being added to their injury list, which must have looked like the roll call at a big-city hospital: Marty Lyons, Reggie McElroy, Joe Fields, Freeman McNeil. It was a disaster for head coach Joe Walton, who was having trouble just trying to find enough bodies to put on the field from week to week. He even started resigning players he had released earlier, signing free agents whom he wouldn't have considered under normal circumstances.

So the Jets almost certainly had to be eliminated as a Super Bowl contender in the American Conference. The New England Patriots, who had been the conference champions the year before, only to be slaughtered in Super Bowl XX by the Bears, had injuries, losing key players like linebacker Andre Tippett and wide receiver Irving Fryar, not to mention having to deal with allegations of drug abuse involving many of their players. The Seahawks, who had beaten us earlier in the season, had gone on to lose five straight, which all but wrote them off as a playoff team. The Miami Dolphins, with quarterback Dan Marino rewriting his own team and league passing records, proved to be amazingly weak on defense and took themselves out of the race. The Raiders proved that losing to us early in the season had not been an upset. Without Marcus Allen, or with a subpar Marcus Allen, the obvious weakness at quarterback (aging Jim Plunkett had lost too much and young Marc Wilson never had too much) would keep them from the playoffs.

So what teams were left? Cleveland, for one, and the Browns were really getting good. We had played them the year before, and even though we lost because Eric Schubert, our kicker then, missed a chip shot in the final seconds, they had become a legitimate force with a tough offense, a brilliant young quarterback named Bernie Kosar and a rough defense. Still, it wasn't as good as our unit (nobody is), and this one had a few question marks in its secondary. But it was good enough, maybe more than just good enough. The head coach was a young, defense-oriented guy, Marty Schottenheimer, who had polished his ideas as an assistant on the Giant staff when Bill Arnsparger was head coach, and Arnsparger is one of the great defensive coaches in the history of the game.

And then there was Denver.

By that time of the season, most people figured the Broncos to be the American Conference favorite to get to the Super Bowl. And now they were in East Rutherford, New Jersey, on November 23. It was their second game of the season in Giants Stadium, since they had been whacked around by the then-healthy Jets, 21–6. The Jets share Giants Stadium with us, and that Bronco ass-kicking had taken place just four games earlier. They remembered what it was like, and their head coach, Dan Reeves, had not exactly fallen in love with our local fans. He said that during the Monday night game with the Jets he had heard some of the most foul language and some of the worst four-letter words he had ever heard coming from the stands in any stadium in the country. "I guess they must teach their kids that stuff in school," he said. (I don't think he should have said those things. Some of our guys had a few four-letter words of their own for coach Reeves, like "sack" and "loss.")

We played strong defense, got a couple of sacks, which is great against that damned Elway, who runs around better than any quarterback I've ever had to play, and we held the running game to 80 yards. Do you know, 51 of them belonged to Elway, who kept escaping sacks all day by just getting out of the way in the last fraction of a second. I'll say this much: He is the most aggravating little bastard in the world because he runs so well and big guys like me get so damned tired by the second half. I just hope I never have to play against John Elway again. Ten years would be too soon. He just runs and scrambles and gets out of trouble. I was exhausted after that game. He's absolutely the best quarterback I've ever played against. I'm just glad we don't have to see him twice a year. (Funny, but the way things would turn out, twice is exactly how many times we'd wind up playing them, but that was still to come.)

I'm sure that if we hadn't been in better shape than any other team in the league, that game could have turned into a defeat. As it was, we needed "Son of Miracle Pass" to put Allegre in position to win another cliffhanger, 19–16, with a 34-yard field goal with 0:06 remaining.

The field goal was great, sure, but how we set it up was another sensational piece of work by Simms, who once again called on his new teammate, Lady Luck.

A lot of people said the AFC didn't have any really good teams in the second half of the season, but I didn't agree with that. I thought the Browns and the Broncos were the two teams to count on. People said the game we played the Redskins for the NFC championship, or the one we played the Forty-Niners the week before in the semifinal round—either one amounted to a Super Bowl, or a better game than the Super Bowl would be. They were right, but only because that's how it worked out. I can't believe it. I had nothing but great respect for Denver and Cleveland, although I have to admit that when we played the Broncos during the season, they didn't play as well as what we had seen on videotape. Maybe we had something to do with that.

Even so, I thought both teams played extremely tough and sound football, and I gained new respect for them.

This one was a toe-to-toe punch-out. With about five-and-a-half minutes left in the game, we were holding on desperately to a 16–9 lead. The Broncos took over on their 27, and in nine plays Elway put them in the end zone. Now there were two minutes to play, the score was tied and it looked like there was no way we could escape a sudden-death period this time. That meant our winning streak and our share of first place in the East would be riding on that, too.

From our 29 Phil put the ball in play, tried a pass to running back Tony Galbreath and it was incomplete. On second-and-ten a defensive end named Freddie Gilbert broke past right tackle Karl Nelson to drop Simms for a disastrous 11-yard sack. Now, on third-and-21 from our own 18, Denver called a timeout to send in a new defense. The clock showed a minute-and-a-half remaining. Simms dropped into shotgun formation and the crowd got real quiet, although I think most of them were already moaning about the end of the winning streak and what was going to be our first home loss of the season. But there must have been others who were thinking that, just maybe, another miracle could happen, another piece of history to remember about this incredible season.

It did. Simms found Bobby Johnson, hero of the Viking game, with a 24-yard completion down the middle of the field, moving the ball from our 18 to our 42. There was new hope. The Denver defense ever so slightly—almost unnoticed unless you knew what to look for—began to sag.

Morris ran for seven, but on second-and-three a holding call on Nelson drew a flag and a ten-yard penalty. Second-and-13 now. Time running out, 57 seconds left. The Broncos then lined up in a decoy zone defense, which our offense had seen on videotape once before. They wanted the offense to think it was going to be zone coverage. They wanted us to call that kind of pattern because when the ball was snapped, they'd go into man-to-man and give Phil no place to throw the ball. So Parcells and offensive coordinator Ron Erhardt took a chance. They guessed it was a decoy, and sent McConkey deep down the middle of the field beyond the zone coverage, into an area where there might be some confusion as to who had to cover him. The pattern was called Fly Left Up. McConkey hauled it in at the Broncos' 25, and ran ten more yards to the Denver 15 before they were able to pull him down. I think the guys who finally stopped him were the two he had split, cornerback Steve Wilson and safety Tony Lilly. Phil and Phil had turned the third-and-21 grave into a first down on the Broncos' 15 with 28 seconds to play. Simms fell on the ball on the next play to eat up some time. Then he fell on it again. And on third down, in a repeat of the Minnesota game's last seconds, Allegre came on to try for a 34-yard field goal. No problem. Smack through the uprights. With six seconds left in the game, we had a 19–16 victory.

We had pushed our record to 10–2, the winning streak

(Photo: Jerry Pinkus)

The team photographer at LSU had me pose as a quarterback dropping back to pass.

Celebrating after a sack during a LSU game. (Photos: LSU Sports Information Office)

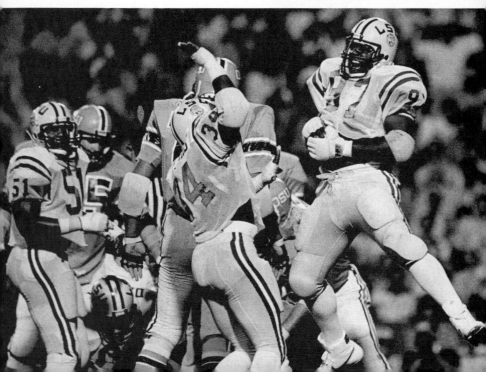

One of the most important men in my professional career, Giants' defensive line coach Lamar Leachman, shown here calmly discussing the situation. (Photo: Jim Reme)

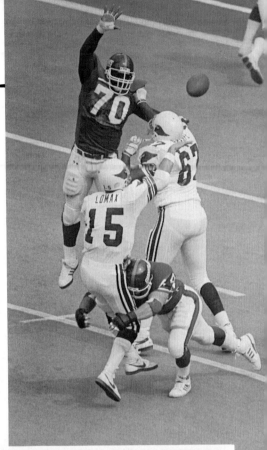

Most often I try to get the quarterback, but in this game against St. Louis (above), it was my job to occupy offensive tackle Luis Sharpe while my teammate, nose tackle Jim Burt, finished off quarterback Neil Lomax. In the photo below, I have spread my blockers and am zeroing in on Atlanta quarterback Steve Bartkowski. (Photos: *Giants Newsweekly*)

Now we're talking. In the photo above, I've corralled Tampa Bay running back James Wilder, one of the best I've ever had to stop, while my teammates Lawrence Taylor (56) and Elvis Patterson (34) lend a hand. Below, I've got my arms wrapped about Philadelphia quarterback Randall Cunningham, and the next thing he's going to hit is the ground. (Photos: *Giants Newsweekly*)

Here I am with my father-in-law, Gaetano DiNapoli, (above) in the backyard of our home, while Annette is seated with my mother, Nellie, at our engagement party (below).

◄ *opposite page:*
I'd like you to meet my wife, Annette DiNapoli Marshall. (Photo: *Giants Newsweekly*)

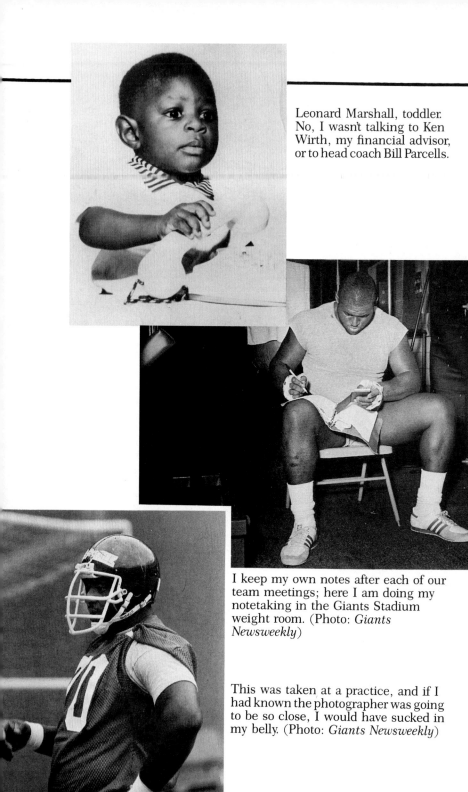

Leonard Marshall, toddler. No, I wasn't talking to Ken Wirth, my financial advisor, or to head coach Bill Parcells.

I keep my own notes after each of our team meetings; here I am doing my notetaking in the Giants Stadium weight room. (Photo: *Giants Newsweekly*)

This was taken at a practice, and if I had known the photographer was going to be so close, I would have sucked in my belly. (Photo: *Giants Newsweekly*)

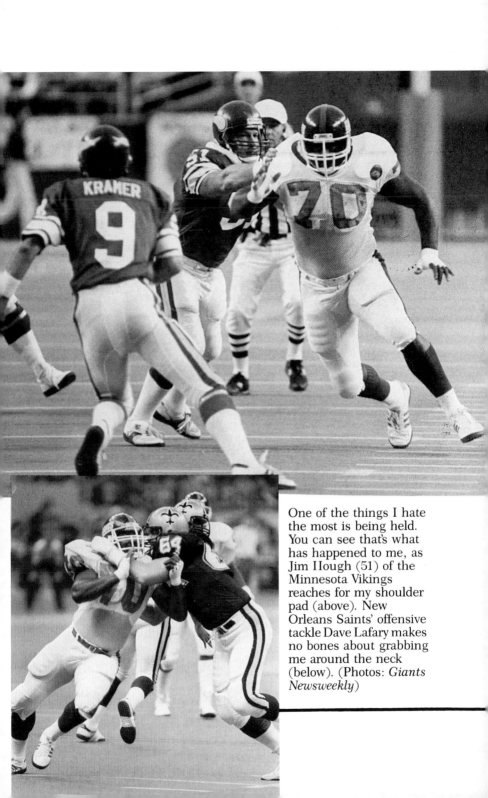

One of the things I hate the most is being held. You can see that's what has happened to me, as Jim Hough (51) of the Minnesota Vikings reaches for my shoulder pad (above). New Orleans Saints' offensive tackle Dave Lafary makes no bones about grabbing me around the neck (below). (Photos: *Giants Newsweekly*)

Some guys chase women.
Not me, I chase
quarterbacks. You can see
me going after a pair of
7s—Joe Theismann of the
Washington Redskins
(above) and Boomer Esiason
of the Cincinnati Bengals
(below). (Photos: *Giants
Newsweekly*)

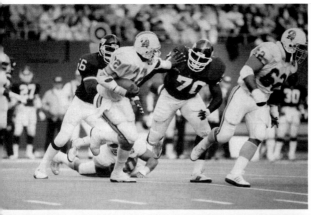

Just fooling around with some of my teammates as L. T. and I move in on Tampa Bay's James Wilder (above), Ron Jaworski of the Philadelphia Eagles (center) and nose tackle Jim Burt (64) and I finish off a Dallas Cowboy (below). (Photos: *Giants Newsweekly*)

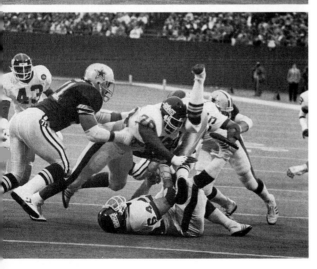

My favorite time in any game—when I've squarely pinned a quarter-back—in this case Jeff Kemp of the San Francisco Forty-Niners. (Photos: *Giants Newsweekly*)

opposite page: ▶
The Forty-Niners are trying to make a Marshall sandwich, with tackle Bubba Paris (77) and guard John Ayres (68) applying the slices of bread. I'm afraid they won this battle—but if I was double-teamed, who got through? (Photos: *Giants Newsweekly*)

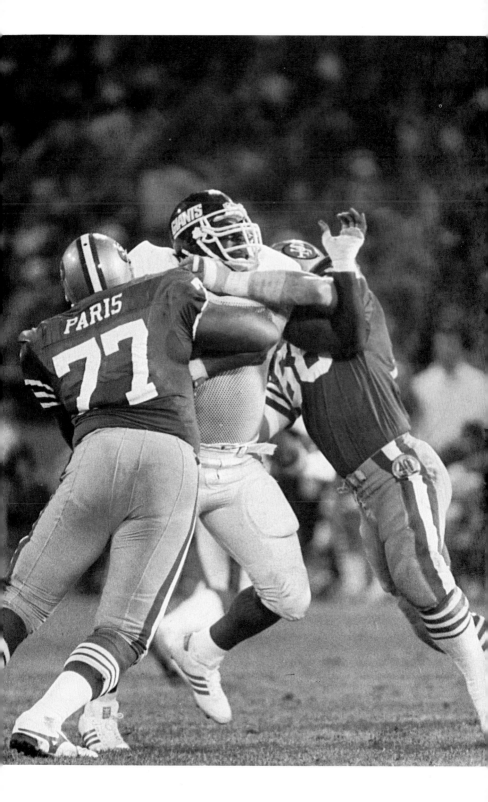

This is what you work for, practice for, study for, and sweat for—the chance to play in the Pro Bowl. This was the 1986 game, when five of us were voted to make the trip to Hawaii. That's me on the left, with Harry Carson (53), L. T. (he wore 58 in this game), Phil Simms (11), and Joe Morris (20). (Photos: *Giants Newsweekly*)

That's Washington Redskin defensive end Dexter Manley (72) following me through the line in Pro Bowl action (below). (Photo: *Giants Newsweekly*)

The 1986 Giants team. (Photo: Jerry Pinkus)

I guess you might say this was how I felt the day we clinched the NFC championship and knew we were going to play in the Super Bowl. (Photo: Jim Reme)

was five, and we had to go to San Francisco the next week for a Monday night game. But by then, nobody thought we'd ever lose again. I mean, the things we had been doing were just so phenomenal, so spectacular, we knew we had something special by the tail.

CHAPTER 8

"They just kicked our asses in the first half because the whole idea of Joe Montana coming back from spinal surgery blew our minds, intimidated us."

EAST MEETS WEST

This was our third Monday night game of the season, and Mondays are always more difficult when you have to travel across the country. Just being on the road is an inconvenience, although some of the guys really look forward to it for reasons like women and getting away from their homes and families for a little while. Others have friends and family in certain cities, and it's a good chance to see people for a quick weekend.

I love it when we go to New Orleans, for instance, because that's where I'm from. My parents and brothers and sisters live there, and so do a lot of my oldest friends, and I usually get permission from coach Parcells to stay a day after the game so that I can visit.

Often when we check into a hotel on a Saturday afternoon there are girls just sitting in the lobby, waiting for us to get in. I don't mean hookers or hustlers, I mean girlfriends. You know, a player will be in some city in the off-season on business or something, and he'll meet this chick, or chicks. So he tells them the team's schedule, says that if he makes the team he'll be in on whatever date and the girls will come by to check him out.

Come on, we're all grownups here, right? Sometimes those girls will stay for the weekend, right in the same hotel in another room, and the player will wait until after curfew check is taken and then spend the night. There have been nights when the assistant coach in charge of checking the rooms does his thing and then as soon as his elevator door closes, ten or fifteen room doors open and players are running for the steps. Or if you can't wait, you tell your roommate that you have a friend in another room and you're gonna be gone all night, and to cover for you when they do bed check.

Most of the Giants are put up two to a room, but I don't have a roommate anymore. I did for a while. He was Kevin Belcher, a guard drafted the same year I was and then moved to center. Man, the Giants really thought they had something, because in his second year, 1984, he became one of the best centers in the league. I remember coach Parcells saying that Kevin was the first center he had ever coached who could be assigned the job of pulling and getting a defensive end, or even a cornerback. He was that quick, and it looked like he took to the position naturally.

The winter after that season, though, he was in an automobile accident in Pennsylvania, where he had been visiting some friends, and injured his upper right thigh. All the nerves had been severed, and Kevin found out he'd never be able to play football again. I can imagine how devastated he must have been, even watching us go through last season and then into the Super Bowl. I guess he figured it could have been him at center instead of Bart Oates. Sad.

My next roommate was defensive tackle Jerome Sally, and that just didn't work out. Then it was Elvis Patterson, who kept the television on all night and the lights on, and talked all the time on the telephone. At the end, I was supposed to room with Joe Morris, but that got screwed up somehow, so I asked Bill Parcells if I could just room by myself.

He said it was no problem, and I'm very happy with the situation now. The Giants are good like that, taking care of the little details that can start to bother somebody and distract his mind from the game. Now I can turn the television off when I'm ready, turn on a light and read if I can't sleep, and tell the hotel switchboard to hold all the calls after a certain time. I'm a private person in a lot of ways. I don't really like the idea of a roommate. I'll talk to Annette before I go to bed and then I don't want to be bothered.

Being on the road, sleeping in strange beds—or with strange women—doesn't help keep athletes in their best game-playing condition. You're not eating the kind of food you're used to, and you just aren't as comfortable as you can be in your own house. There are also distractions and phone calls that you wouldn't get at home. One thing I like, though, is the group of tours for fans that started about three years ago. It's a company called Flower Tours, run by two women, Rose and Carole, and they must be doing really well because it seems they have a big group waiting in every hotel. It's nice, like getting a little bit of home, you know? They're your fans and they're there to root for you to win, and I know they spend a lot of money just for the weekend trip. People don't realize how much things like that can really help. I know some of my team-mates think it's a pain in the ass, but they really do some good for the players. It's just another example of why Giant fans are the best in the country.

Anyway, we had to go to San Francisco for our third Monday night game, and it isn't like the league gave us easy Monday opponents. First we went to Dallas, then we played Washington and now we had to go all the way out there to play the Forty-Niners. I guess our ratings were really good even before we won the Super Bowl.

The Giants hadn't won out west in five games, not since 1975, when we beat the Forty-Niners 26–23 to end a 5–9 season. Since then, the Forty-Niners had won four in a row in Candlestick Park, including semifinal playoff games in 1981 and 1984.

By now we had built our winning streak to five, the second time during the season we had won that many in a row. The first streak had ended in Seattle, and, to tell the truth, I was afraid the second one was going to end in San Francisco. I was more afraid of that game, at least before it started, than at any other time all season. The Forty-Niners are so explosive. They can smack you in the head with a couple of fancy plays and suddenly you're two touchdowns behind and your head is spinning. Then they start with all that unusual fancy passing and guys flying down the sidelines. The Forty-Niners, at least in the years I've played against them, are the best at taking advantage of a lead and putting a team away. They know how to go for the "kill shot" and make it work.

Also, when you think of it, our scores hadn't been exactly spectacular. We had won those five straight by a total of only 18 points, and eight of our ten victories had been by seven points or less. It had been a combination of an outstanding defense, Joe Morris running his ass off and Phil Simms (still getting no respect, being underrated along with his wide receivers. Mark Bavaro had already established himself as the best tight end in professional football). Some people looked at the winning streak, at the record, and said we were due for a fall because almost everything was so close, because we needed so many clutch plays, so many dramatic endings. I don't know, it just felt comfortable. We were playing our defense, doing things that we needed to do to win, and the offense was coming around. In fact, the offense was a lot better than people had thought.

Joe Morris had a great season for a running back, the

greatest any Giant runner had ever had. And Phil was quietly putting together great statistics, too. I've never known a tougher guy than Phil Simms. He stands there in the pocket and sometimes he gets hit so damned hard— the kind of hits I like to put on a quarterback—and you're sure he's hurt. But he just shrugs it off and jumps up again and yells at his line to block better. I don't know where that stuff started about him not being tough because I don't know anybody tougher.

The way things turned out, that Monday was the right night for him to be tough. And talented. Damned near brilliant. Because they were just kicking our asses in that first half. And we were the New York Giants, the best team in the league. I mean, it was embarrassing.

The Forty-Niners, who had won only seven games at the time, had just gotten back their star quarterback, Joe Montana. What had happened to him was scary, and what could happen to him was even scarier. He had gone through spinal surgery only eight weeks before, and his doctors told him he should never play football again because the next time he hurt his back he could be paralyzed for life. He was told to think of himself as a former quarterback. But not this guy. He has tremendous courage, and just eight weeks later, there he was on the field, thinner, looking weak. To tell the truth, I was terrified that I'd be the one to put him in a goddamned wheelchair for the rest of his life.

But he played with all his usual nerve and talent. He insisted that just because he was under his playing weight and looked sick didn't make him any more likely to get hurt, but it might make him more fatigued early on in a game. In fact, he was healthier now, with less to worry about, than before the operation. At least the operation had fixed what had been giving him all the backaches and pain and numbness.

Just remembering that first half is painful. I'm still

embarrassed, because for one full half of a nationally televised game, the Giant defense looked as bad as the worst team's in the league. They really put it to us with their play-action, draws and screens. We just couldn't play our kind of game on defense. We couldn't go after them and hit them and make them play our style. We were playing their style. The Forty-Niners' game plan was built around simple short stuff. Montana was throwing short sideline passes and short passes over the middle, using a two- or three-step drop. Since he has one of the quickest releases in the league—even quicker than Miami's Dan Marino—and was taking advantage of that short drop to get the ball off without having to hit or get sacked, he had all the time he needed to see what we were doing, where we were going and what kind of craziness we were setting up for ourselves to get screwed by. He was throwing short passes and the receivers were running the ball downfield.

It was a nightmare. We'd gain some yards and have to punt, then they'd move the ball right through us, like we weren't even there. They should have scored even earlier than they did, but Jerry Rice dropped a pass in the end zone and that prevented a touchdown. But they did draw first blood, getting a 30-yard field goal by Ray Wersching with 25 seconds left in the quarter.

The second quarter was even worse. Simms was pressured constantly by the Forty-Niner defense, forcing him to throw the ball away time and again. Finally he rushed a throw, and the safety, Carlton Williamson, made an easy interception at the Forty-Niners' 28. And that's when they started kicking our asses.

I mean, that damned Montana was throwing to guys who were so wide open you thought they were walking onto the field from the bench after the play started. He was just picking us apart because we weren't playing our kind of defense. We were tentative, waiting to see where he was going to throw.

On a third-and-three Montana passed seven yards to tight end Russ Francis, wide open in the middle of the field. On third-and-six he again went to Francis, who this time was wide open at the left sideline for eight more yards. On second-and-seven he found Rice almost all alone on the right sideline for 11. On the next play Rice got ten. Then Tyler swept right end for six, and from the 11 Montana hit Rice for the touchdown in the left corner of the end zone.

It was 10–0, and Montana was making us look like jackasses.

We had a little drive, but a 41-yard field goal by Allegre never had a chance because he slipped on the natural grass. It was a scene that illustrated the kind of first half we were having: Our place kicker sitting in his ass in the middle of the field and the people in the stands yelling and jeering and laughing at us.

The ball went back to the Forty-Niners, and this time it was even more embarrassing. The drive was ruthless and methodical, a slow execution. Not one of their players gained more than nine yards, but five of them gained exactly nine. Another got eight, followed by a gain of seven. Sixty yards in seven plays, and now they were on our one-yard line.

Finally, with just 45 seconds left in the half, Montana faked a handoff to the fullback, Roger Craig—another guy who has always managed to stick it to us pretty good—and we bought it. Lawrence Taylor smashed into the line, as if he forgot his responsibilities on the outside. Montana pulled the ball back, handed it to Rice, who came on an end around in the backfield to his left. Rice took the handoff, not one of us laid a hand on him and he pranced into the end zone.

Another touchdown, and this time even the way the Forty-Niners had scored made us look silly. At halftime they had the easiest 17–0 lead any team had ever got.

Everything they did was working. One man always seemed to be open, sometimes more than one. It was total. Walsh and Montana had undressed us, used us, made us do what they wanted us to do, made us react to what they wanted us to think they were going to do. Even in games when we had been beaten badly, we had never felt so inept, so humiliated.

People always ask me, what took place in the Giant locker room at halftime? Did the coaches scream? Were they really angry? Did we fight, argue? Not much happened, actually. It was more of a strategy session than anything else. The coaches just told us that we had been running defenses that we didn't really need to, and had been trying to anticipate what they were going to do offensively. What we had to do in the second half was to go out and play basic defense, each man attacking the man opposite him. In the first half defensive coordinator Bill Belichick had been over-coaching, getting too fancy, trying to show everybody all the shit we could do. He admitted at halftime that he was wrong. All the defensive assistants agreed we were doing stuff that wasn't necessary. We had the best defense in the league. We just had to go out and make them worry about us. So we stopped overreacting, stopped thinking too much and just went out and started pounding away at the San Francisco Forty-Niners, the way we should have been playing all night.

And Simms got hot. In the second half he completed 13 of 16 passes for 175 yards. In the third quarter alone he hit 11 of 14 for 164 yards and three touchdown passes. Better make that THREE TOUCHDOWN PASSES, in big letters, because he never won a bigger game for the Giants.

Despite that miserable first half, we knew we were going to win, and so did the Forty-Niners. We'd had a couple of games like that, where teams that were leading us just knew we were going to win. New Orleans had been one, St. Louis another. Minnesota seemed to know it. So did

Denver. And now San Francisco. Coaches had started telling their players that in order to get to the playoffs they were gonna have to go through the Giants. We were the team to beat, and we weren't about to roll over. Not for any team, and especially not for those damned San Francisco Forty-Niners.

When the third quarter began, they had the ball, and two times in that first series they were flagged for holding. We were just blowing through at the snap and they didn't have any choice but to hold us. We had come out on the field as the old Giants again, and we were hitting anything that moved, going for blood. We were going to show them how defense is supposed to be played. Go-for-the-throat kind of defense from the hardhat, lunchpail blue-collar guys from New Jersey.

The Forty-Niners punted. They were already dead, they just didn't know it yet.

Simms took over at midfield, and on second-and-ten Mark Bavaro put a torch to the offense. We all went crazy—the Giants on the field, the Giants on the bench and the fans who had made the long trip to be there, the Flower Tours group.

Phil threw him a ten-yard pass over the middle. Bavaro caught it and was hit immediately by the cornerback, Ronnie Lott, who can really stick it to receivers. Then Carlton Williamson took a shot. Then a linebacker. Lott stayed on Mark's back, riding him, trying to take him down, but Mark, who is 6–4, 245, wouldn't go down. He was dragging Forty-Niners with him to the end zone. I swear I could feel the electricity charge through the stadium. Finally Bavaro lost his balance on the San Francisco 18-yard line. He had carried, dragged, pulled and clubbed three Forty-Niners an extra 21 yards after making the catch. A short pass turned into a 31-yard gain.

You know, Mark has a reputation for not saying much to anybody, not even the players. He's not mean or nasty, he's just a very quiet person. He lets what he does on the field talk for him, and he is one tough dude. He has played with a cracked jaw, with broken teeth, with all kinds of bruises, sprains and pulls, and he just quietly goes back in for more whenever he can.

Phil joked afterward that if he hadn't gotten us into the end zone after that play, Bavaro would have killed him. Just twice he remembers Bavaro talking to him on the field during a game. Once it was after Phil had been really laid out by a blitzing linebacker. Bavaro came over, looked down at him and said: "Good hit, huh?" Another time, late in a game in Houston and we had already kicked their asses, Phil called a play and Bavaro shook his head. Phil asked what was wrong. "Run it the other way, I got to get something done with that linebacker," Bavaro said. Now, when a guy doesn't talk much, you try to do what he asks the few times he does say something, you know? Obviously he was having some trouble with a linebacker—maybe they had been pounding on each other all game, or maybe the guy had taken a cheap shot. It happens, and there are ways to get even without getting caught, without being stupid. If you can't get to the guy who's been after you, you go for the guy he plays next to, especially if he's an offensive lineman. Those guys need each other there every week, they get used to each other and if somebody new has to come in it can screw up the whole synch of the line.

I remember in one of our games with Philadelphia, those dogs, a guy was blocking me low from the side, trying to get my knees. I couldn't go after him because he wasn't my man, but I remember complaining to their wide receiver, Mike Quick, when we were going back to our huddle. I told him that this guy was being cheap and something was going to happen. Then I put a really special hit on the quarterback, Ron Jaworski, and while we're on the ground I could hear Quick telling that lineman, "Hey, cut it out, he's gonna kill Jaws. Or me."

Anyway, after Mark's 31-yard tug-of-war, Phil finally got us on the board. On second down, nine yards to go, he sent Morris out of the backfield. It was all so casual that nobody seemed to see him or tried to cover him. Joe caught the pass in the middle of the end zone, and the score was 17–7.

San Francisco ran three plays and had to punt, because we were absolutely barbaric by then. You could tell from the way their offensive linemen were acting, the things they were saying, that they were starting to panic. I've mentioned that this team likes to play dirty, and now they were threatening us, telling us they were going to cut us at the knees, block from behind, hurt us. It was pure bullshit. They were out of the game and they knew it.

Our offense took over on our 29. Simms hit running back Ottis Anderson for 12 yards. He hit Bavaro for 11. On fourth down—imagine, fourth down at midfield and a yard to go—Parcells decides to go for it. Morris gets the ball, slips wide to his right and flies all the way down to the San Francisco 34. Sixteen big, fat, embarrassing yards against the San Francisco defense. We had turned everything around by then. They didn't have a prayer. They could hear their bell tolling. On the next play Simms hit Stacy Robinson, the second-year wide receiver, deep down the right sideline. He fell in. That made the score 17–14.

Phil tells a funny story about what happened right after that. You know, once he gets hot he gets all excited and wants somebody to pat him on the back. He wants something from Parcells. So he trots past him on his way off the field after that second touchdown, and slows down. He's looking at him, waiting for him to say, "Good game, Phil" or maybe "Nice pass, way to go." So what does Parcells do? He looks him right in the eye and says, "Hey, Simms, you still gotta get another one." He sure is a strange guy sometimes.

Meanwhile, we were pounding Montana and crushing

the running backs and chopping offensive linemen. Again the Forty-Niners took the ball and again, after three plays had netted three yards, they had to punt. Our next drive didn't take any time at all. From our 29 the offense flashed downfield. Simms was passing the ball the way he would later in the Super Bowl, like it had eyes. He hit fullback Maurice Carthon for seven, got McConkey down the middle for 14, then from midfield launched a missile that Robinson caught on the one. Ottis dove the middle for the points. It had been a five-play, 71-yard drive, and with 3:41 left in the third quarter, we had a 21–17 lead. We had scored three times in less than nine minutes and had gained 191 yards in 15 plays.

How was our defense playing by then? Oh, I think the Forty-Niners knew it was a different ballgame long before then. They were sore and bruised and they knew they hadn't been that way in the first half. During the time the offense did all that scoring, the defense had limited the Forty-Niners to a net of five yards in ten plays.

With the exception of our next game, a street fight against the Redskins the next week at their place, the season was just about over. We were going to do it, we were actually going to become division champions with one more win. Imagine, champions.

And before it was all over, champions of what else? Champions of what more?

CHAPTER 9

"When we won that game against the Redskins and locked up the division, all I could think about was the Super Bowl. I knew we were going there, but before we did, I had a feeling we'd have to meet the Redskins again."

THE REDSKINS AND THOSE OTHER TWO

There is a local joke in Washington, D.C., when the real people, the civilians, are talking about their beloved Redskins: "The largest season-ticket holder is the General Accounting Office, but don't tell the President because he's still buying scalper tickets from Richard Nixon."

RFK Stadium is right next to the ghetto area that government officials deny exists, down East Capitol Street near the Armory Building. By comparison with most other stadiums today, it is small, seating less than 56,000, and most of those seats are taken by the politicians who don't see the slums because they show up in their limos and leave the same way, early, to meet each other later at the swanky restaurants that are as much a part of Washington, D.C., as the poverty-stricken blacks who make up more than ninety percent of the population of our nation's capital and who help to make Washington first in war, first in peace and first in crime in the streets.

This was the setting for the "icing" game of our season, because if we could beat the Redskins for the second time, and on Pearl Harbor Day, we would all but lock up the NFC Eastern Division championship. The first tie-breaker is head-to-head competition, so even if we got surprised in one of our last two games, against weak teams like St. Louis and Green Bay, finishing the season tied with the Redskins at 13–3 or 12–4 would still get us the title based on two victories against them in two meetings.

Everybody, especially the expert writers and television guys, predicted that this was going to be a difficult game, maybe our toughest of the season. The Redskins, who sincerely believed that they had done "everything right but win" in the Monday nighter in New Jersey, were primed for this one on their home turf. When it really gets to rocking, the crowd in RFK is an outdoor version of the Seattle Kingdome. Give them the slightest reason to yell and they can make noise enough to make that old stadium shake and bake and vibrate. It's eerie.

To tell the truth, I had been more afraid of the San Francisco Forty-Niners the week before. The Redskins are a great, tough team, with a whole collection of big old guys who can step all over your face. They are guys like us: Rough and mean and basic. But we know what to expect. We know that it's going to be physical, and that's okay. But the Forty-Niners do all that weird crap nobody can prepare for, so you get more uptight about playing them in a big game. I like the Redskins, and I like the kind of games we play against them. It's just honest, old-fashioned football. I was concerned—we all were—but we knew what we had to do. And we knew what the Redskins were capable of doing to us. There are no secrets when the Giants play the Redskins. It all boils down to who's tougher on that day—and meaner.

I remember getting up that morning with a tight feeling. I'm usually pretty tight before a game, don't want to talk to anybody, don't eat breakfast. It's all part of the adjusting process on game day. Some players come in real early and sleep near their lockers. Some don't show up until the time they have to. Some make a lot of noise, some don't make a sound. Lawrence'll come in one and a half hours before a home game, and he'll be yelling and shouting and getting everybody fired up. That's how he gets ready. I just sit around, read the day's game program and try to get myself together inside.

That morning in Washington, I knew how important this game was, and yet somehow I felt a lot better about it than I had the week before in San Francisco. I knew how tough we had become, how hard we were playing. I knew we could match up with any team in the league in power and quickness, and that included the Redskins. As much as I respected them, I honestly didn't think they could beat us if we played our game, our kind of defense.

The Redskins have a defensive end named Dexter Manley, a great athlete with lots of skills and a knack for being able to beat his blocker and sack the quarterback. The half-circle scar on his cheek he says is a souvenir from a broken bottle during a barroom brawl in Oklahoma City. Manley, a sack specialist, had been shut down by offensive tackle Brad Benson in our first game in the Meadowlands. But during the week leading up to this crucial game, Dexter talked to whoever in the media would listen, and declared: "I'm going to have at least two sacks by halftime, and one of them is going to hurt Phil Simms."

My man Benson took it all quietly: That's his way. But finally, somebody asked him what he thought about Dexter. "I guess I have to say that if he's a sack specialist, then maybe it's a good thing for Phil that I'm an anti-sack specialist," Benson said. "Or maybe I'm just the kind of specialist who specializes in taking out other specialists, you know?"

In any case, Dexter Manley got nothing, which is just what the Redskins got in the sack department: nothing. By the third quarter we had a 24–7 lead. The politicians and officials had started to make their plans for dinner and drinks, the real fans were filing out into the mean streets and we had won a championship.

Well, not officially, but we had it and we knew it, and the Redskins knew it. Finally, after three decades, a season was going to end with the New York Giants heading a list of teams.

The most amazing thing to me is that we played so well against that great offensive line and that I did so well against Jacoby and Grimm. Lawrence had three sacks, I had one, and on two of his, I blocked down on Jacoby to seal him off. I remember when I first came into the league, I was in awe of those two; I thought they were absolutely the best pair of offensive linemen playing next to each other on any team in the league. The first year or two, I was lousy against them. But now I was doing my job and taking an inside move to tie them both up. Now and then they'd say something about the good job I was doing against them, and that was almost as satisfying as winning the game. Man, when that one was over, I didn't need the airplane to fly home. That entire day was a real high.

That game, for the first time during the season, showed another advantage to our end of the line—the Leonard Marshall–Lawrence Taylor side of the defense—that had not been obvious before, at least to the fans. We made the quarterback, Jay Schroeder, concentrate more on us than on his receivers. When he went back to pass and lost sight of L. T., he got very nervous, and started looking around for him, taking his eyes off his receivers. When that happened, I had more time to beat Jacoby or Grimm, Lawrence had time to get into the backfield and we sim-

ply took away their passing game. We knew they weren't
going to be able to run on us (even if they did gain 73
yards, almost three times what they had on the ground
the first game). We knew they had to pass. And once we
made that impossible, we knew we had the game. Without time to set up and with none of his receivers getting
clear deep, Schroeder dumped off the ball on short passes,
making an instant hero out of a rookie named Kelvin
Bryant, who caught 13 passes for 130 yards. But we
intercepted him six times, with six different guys, and
hurried him into a dozen near-interceptions that turned
into harmless incompletions.

The Redskins knew they were beaten by early in the
third quarter. You could tell by the way they were playing.
It was over and we had to fight with ourselves not to
celebrate before that final buzzer.

It was over, and two weeks later, after we blasted out
one-sided, record-setting victories against the Cardinals and
Packers, so was the season. We beat St. Louis, 27–7, and
then, on a Saturday at home, we hammered the Packers,
55–24, winning our ninth straight of the season, scoring
three touchdowns in the first quarter, which established a
team record.

In the locker room after that game—and I remember it
as clearly as if it happened this morning—Lawrence looked
over at me from his adjoining locker and he said, "You
know, we got three games to play, we still got three to go
before I can play golf."

We really were that confident about going all the way.
The playoff games were going to be played in our stadium,
and as long as we kept winning we wouldn't have a single
road game until we went to the Super Bowl. We had
finished the season with the best record in the National
Conference—in the entire league, for that matter—and
that gave us home field advantage for our playoff games.

We hadn't lost a game at home all season. We were playing the best football we had played all year. It just wasn't logical to think we'd be stupid enough to let ourselves get beat by any other team after coming as far as we had.

Were we confident? Sure we were, and with reason. But not confident enough to be stupid. Coach Parcells made sure of that, and he yelled at us that whole week like we were some dumpy team just trying to win one before the season ended. I finally understood why he had kept the lid on us all year, why he never really started bragging about us in the newspapers, even when we kept winning game after game. He was afraid we'd do something to lose, some silly thing that comes from being overconfident, and he knew we still had some games to play.

There's a saying that when the playoffs start, only one team is going to win its last game. And that's the Super Bowl. And that's exactly where we knew we were going. It didn't matter whom we played. Our first opponent in the playoffs was San Francisco, and just a month earlier we had embarrassed them at home, and on national television, with that second-half comeback. So we knew they were coming to New Jersey angrier than ever, but so what? We knew what the Forty-Niners could do, and we weren't all that frightened of them anymore.

One of our offensive linemen, either Chris Godfrey or Billy Ard, I forget which, had a line in one of the newspapers that made a lot of sense to me. Some writer was asking what happened to the Forty-Niners in that Monday night game, and the answer was: "They shut down their motor fifteen minutes too early."

Now we were starting to get down to figuring out how to keep them from ever starting their motor in this playoff game. And despite everything we said, everything the coaches told us, we were all, I'm sure, secretly waiting for the chance of a rematch with the Chicago Bears.

We had waited a full year for that to happen.

CHAPTER 10

ALL THAT GLITTERS . . .

Lord, there are more ways a pro football player can get his ass in trouble in this New York metropolitan area than I think I want to know. That's true even when you aren't looking for anything. If you're out shopping, the sky's the limit and nothing is too difficult for one of the hustlers to take care of. On the other hand, the sky's the limit for what you are risking, and for what can happen to you if you get in trouble, legal or otherwise.

Not too long ago, Annette and I were in a comedy club in New Jersey, and while we're sitting at the bar waiting for our table, this guy comes over. Nice guy, well dressed, friendly and smiling and all that. We're talking about football, about the Super Bowl, about all the stuff that fans like to talk about—and it's okay, man, they're entitled. Sometimes it's a pain in the ass, but I'd rather everybody knows who I am and what I'm about and that I'm one of the local heros, you know? I kind of dig being known.

So anyway, we're talking and having a pretty good time and then they call our name out and tell us our table is ready. So we get up to go, and the guy shakes my hand, then he gives me one of his business cards.

"Hey, Leonard," he says, "if you ever need some party stuff, you know, just give me a call, it'd be my pleasure. No charge, either, man. You're one of the Giants."

Party stuff? He meant drugs. Cocaine. I didn't know what to say, but Annette took the card out of my hand and right in front of him she tore it up into small pieces and dropped them on the bar.

You want that stuff? It's easy. There are guys in North Jersey and New York City who live for the time when somebody asks them for something, when a sports celebrity or somebody from entertainment or politics wants a favor. And sometimes they are your best damned friends, too, "Oh, sure, Leonard, here, take this car—no, I don't care when it comes back. Or if it comes back. It's cool, man, just enjoy."

Or sometimes they come up to you in restaurants, in the parking lot outside the stadium, and they try to give you stuff. Real stuff, expensive shit, "Hey, Leonard, here, take this watch, man, it's a Rolex." "Here, how about a little diamond trinket for your girl, Leonard?" "What about a nice set of wheels? Just call me on Monday morning, man, any kind of car you want, you understand? Guy like you, you shouldn't be driving around in something cheap, you know?"

Do I ever talk with them? Sometimes, but only until I get a feel for where they're coming from. Do I ever take their stuff, their "gifts"? Hell, no, my momma didn't raise no stupid children. I have so much to lose that I'd have to have my head examined. I'd have to be stone-cold crazy to even think about it. I like what I do too much, I like who I am and I am very concerned with my image, not just now while I'm a football player but for the rest of my life. I'm clean and I'm gonna stay that way.

Other guys? Well, that's for them to talk about. I know

stuff. I know what some players do and have done—not on the Giants necessarily, but on other teams. I'm aware of what goes on. And see, there are guys who don't mean anything by it when they try to give you things. Maybe they're rich guys, and it makes them feel important to tell their friends, *"Hey, Leonard Marshall is wearing one of my watches,"* or *"Carl Banks drives one of my cars,"* or *"Joe Morris, man, he's going on vacation to the Caribbean for a couple of weeks and staying in my hotel."* I guess you could make a point that there isn't really anything wrong with that kind of thing.

But you never know what kind of guy you're dealing with. Suddenly the guy who gave you the $15,000 watch is on the phone a year later "just wondering" how much it would take to get me to lay down and let a running back go past me, or to find a way to "trip" and miss sacking the quarterback so he can get the pass off, see? You take something, anything, from one of those guys and you are going to find nothing but grief coming from it.

Now, everybody has friends, and some of those friends own businesses, or can do things, and that's different. Hey, I get a good deal on appliances, television and stereo stuff through one of Ken Wirth's good friends. But I pay. Maybe I don't pay full retail prices but I pay, and nobody has a claim on anything else. I have some friends who own automobile dealerships, and I get good deals when I want to lease a new car, or buy one. I bought my father a car, a Pontiac, and it was from a guy I met when I first lived in Jersey City. Nothing wrong with our deal, and there's nothing suspicious about our relationship. He's a Giant fan and I buy him tickets. Buy them. And he gives me a good deal on cars. So I figured I'd buy my daddy a car and my friend arranged for him to pick it up at an agency near home. I'm his buddy and we go out together and talk to each other on the telephone and yeah, I get him tickets. So what?

Game tickets are like magic words. Everybody wants tickets, and nobody can get them because the Giants sell out every game—all but the few seats they keep aside for their friends, the players and the visiting team. There's a waiting list for season tickets, with more than 15,000 names on it. Some of these people are going to have to live to be 2,000 years old before they get a chance to buy season tickets. But the players get tickets. We each get two for each game, and we can buy two or four more. It's a monster problem for me when we go to play in New Orleans because all my friends and relatives want to go to the game. Sometimes I'll get like fifty, sixty requests. So I ask other players who don't have any people in that city to buy as many as they can for me, and I'll return the favor when we get to Chicago, or Dallas, or someplace where they need a lot of tickets.

The absolutely craziest I've ever seen the ticket situation was when we knew we were going to the Super Bowl. Each player on the participating teams gets to buy twenty-five tickets at face value. Do you know what that means? The tickets sell for seventy-five bucks a shot, and that's if you're a senator or a judge or the president of General Motors. Average people, the guys in the street? They don't have a chance. The league office handles distribution and sale of tickets, and I swear I don't know where they go. Each team in the National Football League gets like 1,500, the two teams in the game get 15-20,000 and the team in the city where the game is being played gets 10,000. (Last year the Rams and the Raiders were both the "home city" teams, so the league accommodated them by cutting back on the allotment.) The league people have to save a lot of tickets for the advertisers, the networks, the special people who help them all year. And then there's the usual allotment set aside for the media—the newspaper, magazine, radio and television people covering the game.

All of a sudden there aren't any tickets left and now

everybody in New York and New Jersey wants to go. I don't know how travel agencies get all their tickets, but there are lots of advertisements in the papers and on the radio for trips to the Super Bowl for package prices. I guess they buy tickets from the season-ticket holders who don't want to go but don't mind making a nice little profit.

Here's the way it works. Say a guy has season tickets, but he lives in New York and he has to work and he can't really afford the trip anyway. So he picks up his two tickets, pays the face value and then sells them to a ticket broker for like double the money. Quick and easy—a little extra cabbage for the family dinner table.

Now the broker has two tickets that originally cost $150 for the pair, but he paid $300. No problem. He sells them for $500, $750, $1,000, even more. A friend who called me before our Super Bowl told me he had to have a pair of tickets, and would be willing to pay me $2,000 apiece. I told him he was crazy, absolutely nuts. I told him he could get the finest hotel suite, have room service bring up caviar and champagne, order full-course steak dinners, with a beautiful woman under each arm, watch the game on one of those monster television screens and he still wouldn't be spending $4,000. The game just isn't worth it. No game is—not for that amount of money.

But everybody wants tickets, and there isn't anything wrong with wanting them. If people have the money, there are always tickets to be had, I guess. All I know is the Giants are always sold out and I don't think that would be any different if there were 100,000 seats in Giants Stadium instead of 75,000. If I can help friends or relatives get tickets, I do. But I never scalp them, for the same reason that I won't take anything from anybody I don't know. It just isn't worth it. I'm the only one in that arrangement with anything to lose, and I know just how much. The other guy? He's just looking for an edge, a favor or maybe a customer. No deal, I'm not interested. It's easy for a player to get into financial trouble, no matter how much money he makes. All he's got to do is spend it on the wrong things. For instance, sometimes a guy might blow his entire $10,000 playoff check on a custom-made fur coat.

Last time I thought about it, I wasn't able to come up with a way where a fur coat could earn a guy interest on his money, or let him put a down payment on a piece of real estate. I mean, there are guys with five cars, with $10,000 coats and gold chains, with $2,500 suits. Why? What's the point of all that? I always figured it was smarter to save the money, bank it, get interest, let it work for you. Nobody needs five cars. That's like giving a little kid a suitcase full of cash and telling him he can buy whatever he wants.

You know, from the time a football player gets into college, he doesn't have to do a damned thing for himself. All his transportation and hotel reservations are arranged for him. He puts some stuff in a suitcase and somebody else takes it to the hotel for him. All he has to do is show up on time and play the game. I know players who have given their agents full authority over their money. They get all their bills paid by the agent. He makes all the investments, all the decisions, and sends them an "allowance" each week. They enjoy having someone else handling all their affairs.

There are guys playing in the National Football League who have never written a check, never paid a bill, not even an electric bill or rent. They don't know the first thing about money, either how to spend it or how to manage it or who to hire to do a good job for them. It's amazing to me that people can be so unconcerned with their money. For almost every one of the players in this league, their salary represents the most money they're ever going to make at one job. I mean, there are guys who just know football, who went through college without really paying attention, who were passed through because they were football stars.

So when football is over, those guys don't have another job waiting for them. They can't become proficient in something else because they aren't trained to be professionals in anything else. It's sad but true that most pro football players can't get an average job when they return to the real world again.

If they realize this, they can turn it to their advantage. If they spent four or five years in college just preparing to be football players, then they should know enough to plan ahead. For most of them, it's curtains when they retire. But it doesn't have to be that way, not if a guy utilizes the assets he has as a ball player, not if he establishes contacts, markets himself. Not many players do this. On the other hand, there are image guys, who are marketable in a certain city or region and who are really going to make it after football is over.

I know I'm going to live in New Jersey for the rest of my life. I love it here. I'm close enough to New York City without having to put up with all the bullshit of living there. This is where I have to stay, because as long as there is Wall Street and those two big towers (the World Trade Center) there is going to be money and investment opportunities and that's where you'll find Leonard Marshall.

Now, if Mel Blount walks into a restaurant or an office building in Pittsburgh, people are going to know who he is. The same goes for Terry Bradshaw, Lynn Swann, Franco Harris, Donnie Shell, Fats Holmes, L. C. Greenwood, Jack Ham, Jack Lambert, Dwight White. And in many cases the recognition factor is more than local. I remember when I met Claude Humphrey, who played a long time ago for the Atlanta Falcons. He was in my town once, when I was a kid, and he was one of the biggest influences in why I do what I do today, because Claude Humphrey was such a gentleman to me, and to so many other kids. To be able to meet a guy like that when I was ten years old was very inspiring. Kids look up to pro athletes. I knew who he was and I knew who Robert Pennywell was, and Jeff Van Note and Billy Ryckman and R. C. Thielemann. I knew who all of them were, and I knew they played for the Atlanta Falcons. We followed Atlanta down there in Franklin as much as we did the Saints.

I think a lot of people will remember who I am because of what we've accomplished with the Giants. It's funny, when I see William Perry make all that money for being so fat, I remember when I was a rookie. I was the biggest joke in town. Leonard Marshall was so fat, they had to weigh him on a truck scale. People are going to remember that. Wherever I go, wherever Lawrence Taylor goes, and Phil Simms, Mark Bavaro, Joe Morris, all the way down the line, there are maybe ten or fifteen players on this team who will always be remembered. I wanted to be on the Oakland Raiders when I was a kid because they were all bad-asses—tough guys like Lyle Alzado, Dave Casper, John Matuszak. But see, they are remembered because they were pro players who acquired an image, a character.

Sometimes, though, you get remembered for the wrong things. When I had that one-day holdout last summer, I knew I was coming back. I knew I'd be signing a contract because I didn't want to turn out like Todd Bell and Al Harris. They were the two starters on the Chicago Bears' team who held out all summer and into the season, insisting on how much they deserved to get, and suddenly the Bears found starters to replace them. Hey, I'll be honest, I remember laughing at them when I read that they screwed themselves out of $72,000 in playoff and Super Bowl money and a ring. And especially, the chance to say that at one time they were members of a championship team. That's real important to me because I was never on any championship teams before. And for me to say that I was on a world championship football team, that's big time. John Madden said when Pat Summerall asked him how he thought Parcells felt after we won: "There's no way to describe it, he's on top of the world." Of course, Madden had won a Super Bowl as a coach, and he knew there's nothing like it. It can't get any better than that.

But it sure can get worse, and not even a Super Bowl ring can guarantee anybody's future. Not being able to handle your money is just another indication of not knowing what to do. That can mean not knowing what to do on the field or in your private life. Responsibility covers a lot of ground.

Players forget things. Sometimes they forget to make a deposit into their checking account. Other times they forget to show up at a place they said they'd be. I got married in April, and I invited a lot of the players. Some of them responded by saying they would not be able to attend. That's okay. But others who said they would be there didn't show—no call, no message, no nothing. Now, I think that's irresponsible. After all, it was an expensive deal—the caterer charged $100 for each setting.

Like I said before, most football players are pampered. When they get ready to go to training camp, their plane tickets are reserved by the club. Their ride to camp is arranged by the club. When they get there they are given an itinerary and they work strictly from that itinerary, like a kid. Everywhere they go, every plan, every step is made for them. All they have to do is show up and do the work. Everything is done by the club. They give you money on the road to buy dinner. All you have to do before a game is buy your dinner. It's nice, but it doesn't give a player a sense of discipline or responsibility. Teams should really drill a player in how to think, how to act, how to take care of his responsiblities.

A lot of players are making $100,000 a year and they're living like it's $500,000. They've got a Porsche, a $2,200 a month apartment, jewelry, furniture, the broads, the night life. There are some guys on the Giants who really spend their money, who really like to spend it. Hey, I spend money, so does Phil Simms and Joe Morris and Carl Banks. We all spend pretty good money. But that's for our homes, families, investments. But more important than anything else is having enough to carry you over the goal line when your playing days are over.

CHAPTER 11

THE RUN FOR THE ROSES

"You know what really got us upset? Those lousy three points that the Forty-Niners got . . . and the fact that we couldn't get Chicago."

I don't think any defense has ever played back-to-back playoff games the way we did against San Francisco and Washington the first two Sundays of the year. These were the two of the four best teams left in the National Conference, so they were supposed to be viewed with respect and a healthy fear. Coach Parcells tried everything he could to make us aware of the downside of being confident, which is overconfidence. That's how upsets happen.

We were so high, on such a roll, and playing at home was the best thing that could have happened to us. People were whipped up into a frenzy they hadn't known for a generation. The last time a Giant team won a championship of any kind had been twenty-five years earlier. We had lived with the names and the memories of those old Giant teams for a long time. Phil Simms said that if we won it all, then maybe the fans would consider us the best Giants team ever, and get rid of all the ghosts.

There was great excitement then, too. The Giants had guys like Y. A. Tittle and Andy Robustelli and Kyle Rote and Frank Gifford. But man, that was a long, long time ago, and the only reason they were so much in every fan's mind a quarter of a century later is that later Giant teams hadn't given them anything to be proud of. Until we came along. It had really started for us two years earlier, when we came back from that 3-13-1 season to be 9-7. When we went out to California and beat the Rams in the wild-card game, people started getting their hopes up, dusted off the old dreams and tried to see if they'd fit our team. That season was disappointing, though, because we lost the next playoff game to the Forty-Niners. We should have beaten them, and we could have, easily. It was 21–10, but our offense just couldn't get anything going. In fact, our only touchdown came when Harry Carson returned an interception all the way. But in our hearts we knew we should have won that game, just as when we lost to Chicago the year after that. We *really* felt we should have won that one. But those games established the groundwork. You know, each team we lost to in a playoff game went on to win the Super Bowl and admitted when things were all finished that we were the toughest team they had played.

I'm not interested in those kind of compliments. I don't want another team to be sitting back and trying to think about which was the toughest team they played, even though they won everything. I like it much better when a team gets beat and the coach tells the writers that the Giants are the toughest team they played all season.

But nobody on earth could have imagined the outcome of that first Sunday of 1987. The Forty-Niners were a good, strong, very smart team. What happened was just a case of things getting out of control too early and then mushrooming. It's probably true that the biggest blowouts happen when two good teams are playing each other because all of a sudden it's a two-touchdown lead, or three touchdowns, and the other guys have to change stuff, have to take chances to get back in the game. And then mistakes happen and the score takes off.

What I'm getting at is that we beat the San Francisco Forty-Niners in the second round of the playoffs by the score of 49–3. Can you believe that? I still can't.

I remember getting ready to leave the house that morning, feeling good but tight, the way I usually feel before a game. I mean, there isn't much else in the world for me to get that worked up about. There are great football players on the other team, no matter whom we're playing, and it's competition at the highest level, man. I've heard people compare football to war. But it's not like that, because when the game is over everybody can be friends. It is, though, the greatest form of competition I know because there's so much on the line—not just money but pride and status.

So you get out there, and it's cold, and the ground is hard as a rock—especially our field—and those guys are on the other side of the line and they're mumbling and growling and yelling. You know that they are going to do the best they can to win this game, and once it gets started, once you are into it, it becomes the most important thing in the world.

Sometimes I think the playing of the game is hypnotic. There are times during a game when a tune comes into my head, and I can get the rhythm and feel the grace of it all. Sometimes I can drift off, sort of, for a series. It doesn't hurt my game because I still do all the things I'm supposed to; playing defensive end is really a subconscious reaction. That's how deep football is in my psyche. Sometimes I'll make all the moves, follow all the assignments, without realizing it or remembering it later. It's like I'm having what they call an out-of-body experience. Yeah, it's scary, a little. It happened a few times in college games, and a few more times since I've been with the Giants.

When I got to the stadium, I was in my game mood. I was tight, tense, real quiet. I wasn't hungry. I just wanted to get someplace in a corner and not talk. I had to think about my assignments and the guys I was going to come up against. Of course, I was also thinking about winning and moving one step closer to the Super Bowl, especially one step closer to the rematch we had hoped for all season with the Bears.

The locker room mood was about the same as it had been all season—nobody any louder than usual, nobody any bitchier than usual. Lawrence was doing his thing, yelling at people, fooling with guys. Most of the other guys were quiet, just sitting on the stool in front of their locker, lying on the carpet, reading the game program, trying to nap or just closing their eyes and listening to the music from our intercom system.

Although everybody knew how important the game was—if we lost, it would waste all the great things we did all season—there was one feeling that hadn't been around every other game during the season: We were truly confident. I mean, there were times when we weren't sure of winning certain games, like maybe that Monday night game against San Francisco, but now we were really very sure of ourselves. We already had that exciting come-from-behind victory in the bank, and we knew they were thinking about it.

But nobody could have expected the outcome. It was just unreal. It was like watching a perfect training film, showing exactly how to do each thing, exactly how to play each position and exactly why the Forty-Niners knew they were in over their heads.

It was 28–3 at halftime. But very early in the first quarter something happened that kind of predicted the way the whole game would go for them. They had put the ball in play on their 37-yard line, and now it was second-and-ten on the 50. Montana dropped back, got the blocking and watched for Jerry Rice to get clear. Did he ever. He ran a straight post pattern down the middle of the field and was wide open. I mean, that sucker was going to score a touchdown. A big one. All Montana had to do was get him the ball. And he did, too. It was a great pass, right in his hands. He caught it and started running and the guys he had split, Elvis Patterson and Herbie Welch, were just chasing because that was all they could do. Rice was gone. Heading for six.

He dropped the ball. It just slid out of his hands. Nobody touched him, nobody bumped him—hey, nobody could catch him. He just dropped the ball, right around our 25. It was electrifying, because the crowd hushed up for a minute, as if in shock, and then started screaming. Rice tried to pick it up but he kicked it into the end zone with Kenny chasing it. And he recovered it, too. We had escaped a disaster, got the ball and you could see the San Francisco guys just droop.

Phil took advantage. He moved the offense from our 20 in for the points in just ten plays, scoring on a pass to Bavaro for 24 yards. I think the Forty-Niners were real tired of seeing Bavaro by then. I mean, he had started the rally out there in December, and now he put the Giants on the scoreboard when he beat two of their backs, Ronnie Lott and Tim McKyer. So it was 7–0, and they took the ball. They moved against us for a while. On third-and-five from our 35, Montana faked a draw to Roger Craig and threw a 20-yard pass to their tight end, Russ Francis. But then we got tougher. Two runs got six yards and on third down we rushed Montana into throwing the ball away, high over the end zone back line. So they took the field goal, and with a 1:20 left in the first quarter we had a 7–3 lead. Would you believe that was all they'd get for the rest of the day?

See, we panicked Montana. In that Monday night game, especially in the first half when they had had everything their way, he had been taking that short two-step drop, throwing on a rhythm, taking away everything Lawrence and I could do. He threw quick out passes and didn't stay in the pocket long enough for us to sack him. His mistake, or coach Bill Walsh's mistake, in the playoff game was trying to do all those other things, dropping back, throwing long, giving us a chance to get to him.

Once we saw how he was going to play the game, there was no way they were going to win. It all blew up in their faces in the second quarter. Herbie Welch intercepted a pass after Banks had pressured Montana into a quick throw, gave it to Elvis on a lateral and he took it 16 yards to their 45. On the very first play Phil gave the ball to Morris, and Joe took it between left guard and left tackle, got great blocking from Brad Benson, Zeke Mowatt and Chris Godfrey and beat their safety, Carlton Williamson, into the end zone. That made it 14–3.

Now they were really sweating and their next series we just beat them down. First their tight end goes in motion and it's a five-yard penalty. Next, Burt nails the halfback, Joe Cribbs, for a one-yard loss. Pepper Johnson whacks Montana, who just gets rid of the ball, but it's incomplete. Then their right guard, Randy Cross, goes in motion. On third-and-21, a short pass to Craig at the right sideline gets them seven yards.

So they punt. We go all the way to their 28 but on third down Tony Galbreath catches a pass over the middle and gets stopped for a nine-yard gain. Okay, field goal, pump up that lead, right? Wrong. My man Parcells is getting to be like a riverboat gambler. Raul Allegre comes in, but it's a fake field goal play. At the snap he goes in motion to his left, like a back. The holder is our second-team quarterback, Jeff Rutledge, and he's already got the ball. So he stands up and throws it to Bavaro for 23 yards.

We're on their five, man. They are really down. Joe scores but Godfrey is called for holding, so it wipes out the touchdown and puts us on their 15. On the next play, Lott drops a sure interception in the end zone. So Phil throws to Bobby Johnson and it's a touchdown and we're up, 21–3. That was with 50 seconds left in the half.

Montana tries it again, and on the second play from scrimmage Burt crashes through the middle of the line and really clocks him. I mean, that poor guy just crumpled, and it was just as he was getting rid of the ball, too. The thing wobbled in the air, short and off target, and Lawrence intercepted it. I gave him the block he needed and L. T. was in the end zone, a 34-yard touchdown.

Now it's really over. In comes another quarterback, Jeff Kemp. The half is over. We were all worried about Montana because he was just lying there on his back, not moving at all. Everybody was thinking about his back and, you know, wow, Burt really did it to him this time.

It turned out all right. I think he had a mild concussion and a whole lot of aches. For him the season was over, and we had a ball in the second half, beating up on their offense, giving them nothing, nothing at all.

I remember one play, a wide run with Russ Francis as the blocking tight end moving out ahead of the runner, Cribbs. Francis is a big, strong man; he's 6–6 and weighs close to 250. He comes head-up to Banks, and Carl picks him up, throws him off to the side and makes the tackle. That was in the second quarter when they were only down 7–3, and that took a lot out of them too.

Carl had one of the best games I've seen, not as good as his Super Bowl performance, but maybe his best up to then. He had seven tackles and he was all over the field.

It was nothing to go on and win it, and after the game Bill Walsh said something I really liked. He said that the Forty-Niners were a good team that played a good game, but lost to a great team that played a great game. I liked that. He said that the Forty-Niners were "shattered" by a great team. The Giants, he said, played a great game right to the end, a perfect game, and he thought we were going to go all the way.

The only fly in the ointment was the fact that the day before the Redskins had upset the Bears in Chicago. So we weren't going to get that rematch after all. Well, if you aren't good enough to keep winning, then you just don't get to play in a championship game, you know? Meanwhile, we were going to have to get ready for a third game against the Redskins.

Nobody expected it to be anything but a tough, tough game—at least nobody on our team did. But the Forty-Niners were still talking about how great a game we played. Jeff Fuller, their veteran safety, said that he didn't see how the Redskins had a chance, and that if we played the next week the way we had just played, he didn't think the Redskins could win.

Parcells was still being careful, though. He said the game was "just one of those things that happen" and that the Redskins were the best team we had played all year. He had had a feeling it would come down to this all along, and it was right that it should come down to them and us for the trip to the Super Bowl.

Me? If somebody had forced me to answer, I would have had to say I was making plans to play on January 25 in the Rose Bowl in Pasadena, California. I didn't think anybody could stop us after that exhibition.

CHAPTER 12

"There was nothing else to do except go to Pasadena, although after that show at the end of the Redskin game, the fans really deserved one more home game. The Super Bowl."

THREE'S A LUCKY NUMBER

I showed up too early for the game against the Redskins, earlier than I have ever showed up for a game. I thought it was a one o'clock kickoff. I was wrong. It was four o'clock. And I had left my house at nine-thirty in the morning.

Looking back, I guess I was a little tight, a little preoccupied. Maybe it's from banging my head too many times, I don't know. Maybe that's why I hear tunes in my head during a game. That tune stuff, though, helps me relax; it keeps me from being tight all the time.

See, there is a lot more for players to learn, not just the quarterbacks, than the public realizes. I mean, we've got fifteen stunts, at least, just for the defensive line. We have at least fifteen different techniques, and each one has a different name and number, let alone all different kinds of blocking schemes. There are at least forty-five different defenses that we use; we have to learn at least twenty-five offensive formations every week.

For the defense alone we get a thousand-page playbook that we memorize at summer camp. Just for defense.

Terminology, other offenses, formations, plays, blocking schemes, individual and group techniques. When a college player is handed a playbook twice as thick as a phone book, all he can say is, damn, how do they expect me to learn all this material so fast?

You don't use it all every week—you review what's necessary to you at the time—but you have to learn it all. See, we may use a defense in the first or second week of the season, and then drop it, and all of a sudden in the fifteenth game we may use it again. That's tough, and it's something a lot of the guys have to learn all over again. We might have to work a little longer at practice, and if I still don't think I have it right, I'll stay late with Lamar and he'll make sure I get it. It's my job, and I have to know exactly what to do. I don't like going into a game uncertain about the smallest thing.

Most teams have complex playbooks and strategies, for both defense and offense, but we do so many different things that our defensive book is probably thicker than most, and a lot more complicated.

From what I hear, Denver's is even worse. Our coaches spent a lot of time in Denver, visiting with their coaches, long before the season started, because we were going to play the teams from the American Football Conference West and we hadn't played too many teams in that division for so long it was a foreign area. But teams do cooperate. Denver helped the Giants' coaching staff by explaining what Seattle does, what the Raiders do, etc. It helps Denver, too, because if the Giants can beat those teams, it's better for the others in that conference. Giant guys gave information to the AFC West coaches on Dallas and Washington too. It works both ways. But our coaches said the Broncos do more shit than any other team they had seen in the league, by far. I mean, they'll figure out a way to put another defensive lineman on the ground and stand a linebacker up in an odd position, or put an end down and put a linebacker here and here, like Chicago does and like Philadelphia is starting to do now. There's a lot to learn, and once you do, you start thinking about other defenses, like you're trying to invent some new formation that would actually work.

Here's my own invention: I'd put in a four-man line with three linebackers and four defensive backs, but I'd organize it so that it looks like the "46" but in a different way. It might look like the old 4–3, too, but it isn't. With the guys on our defense, for instance, I'd take Eric Dorsey and place him at the left end, right over the left guard, to start an unbalanced line. I'd place myself over the center like a defensive tackle, and I'd put Erik Howard next to me over the other guard. I'd have John Washington wide outside the other tackle, and I'd have him float to whatever the open side is.

All right? Now I take two linebackers and stack them in the tight end gap, one over the tight end and the other inside the tight end and the tackle. Lawrence and Banks, on the same side. I'd put Carson or Pepper Johnson in the middle. On one corner I'd put Elvis tight on a receiver, and Perry Williams tight on the other receiver and I'd bring Andy Headen in as strong safety instead of a smaller man. I'd even use Kenny Hill there instead of Headen. And if the receiver was real fast I'd put Mark Collins in place of Elvis, and I'd have Elvis move over and play the position of free safety.

I'd call that Wild Style 61. Now, if the corners jam the receivers, we rush Lawrence and John while Erik and I maneuver into different positions. You notice I didn't put Jim Burt in there. Well, if you're going to a four-man line, you'd want bigger, faster players, like Howard, Dorsey, Washington and myself. But I'll use him as a back-up or in a run situation.

Anyway, it was really nervous time that morning. I'm in the locker room too damned early; only a few of the guys were there. You know, being there that early, practically by yourself helps you concentrate and really get worked up into that game attitude. So I was thinking, here we were, one game away from the Super Bowl, riding a winning streak, playing the best damned defense in the league, getting ready to play a team we had already beaten twice. We were playing just one more game for the right to represent our conference in the Super Bowl. There had been twenty Super Bowls, and the Giants had never been to one. Even the Eagles got there one time, and so did the Jets. I knew how excited the fans were. Man, that was all we had been hearing for the past two months, how the Giants were finally going to the Super Bowl, how they would finally have something to cheer about, and I really believe the fans helped us get there. I mean, they were so worked up, so excited, that it would have been horrible to let them down. I know how loyal they are, but if we had lost that game to the Redskins, that might have been enough reason for even them to give up on us.

Coach Parcells made a good point when he was talking to the writers that week. He was talking about the fans—and he's very careful to mention them, to let them know just how important he thinks they are, how much he values their support. He said that when he gets a letter that starts out with a guy saying he was a long-suffering fan, he throws it out because the guy is complaining. If a letter starts off with the writer saying he's a die-hard fan, though, Bill reads it through. He likes that expression, die-hard. I think it's how he views this team.

What I like to do when I get to the stadium early is different stretching exercises, just make sure everything is warm and loose. The worst kind of day for pulled muscles is when it's real cold, and then you have to do more to get ready, to keep your muscles loose and warm.

That morning was really cold, actually more windy than cold. That wind reportedly gusted up to fifty miles an hour

during the game. I'm not surprised because it sure felt
like that to me. Coach Parcells told Harry Carson, our
team captain, that if he won the coin toss, the Giants
would elect to kick off. That meant we'd have the choice
of which end of the field we wanted to start out on, and
Parcells wanted to take the wind end of the field so we'd
have the wind at our backs. In the Redskins' faces.

It turned out just that way. I mean, it was perfect. That
might have been the only advantage we needed, the way
we were playing. We kicked off and the Redskins started
on their 20 because Allegre's kickoff got caught in that
gale and the ball landed way behind the end zone.

They tried twice running with George Rogers, and Carl
Banks nailed him both times for two-yard gains. A pass
was no good and then the Redskins had to punt. I almost
felt bad for their punter, Steve Cox. He didn't have much
chance, kicking into that wind, and he was able to manage only a 23-yard punt. We scored with that first possession when Allegre kicked a 47-yard field goal—with the
help of the wind. Parcells knew what he was doing.

The wind kept on being a problem for the Redskins.
The next series they had to punt again, and this time that
poor Cox guy got off a 26-yarder—out of bounds on the
Redskins' 38.

We got a big break on that drive. On a third-and-ten
pass, Simms threw low to Manuel, but the officials called
center Bart Oates for holding. Why didn't the Redskins
just refuse the penalty? I'm not sure, but we were on their
26, and we had the wind, so that's only a 43-yard field
goal for Allegre. Again the decision Bill had made at the
start of the game was paying off. Maybe the Redskins'
coach, Joe Gibbs, thought that his defense could hold us
on third-and-20, so he took the penalty and moved us
back to their 36. I had a feeling that Phil was going to find
a way to get the first down, and damned if he didn't. He
threw down the middle, found Lionel Manuel, who had

beaten cornerback Vernon Dean, for a 25-yard gain to their 11. Three plays later Phil hit Bobby Johnson for the points, but our fullback, Maurice Carthon, was flagged for holding. So on the next play he hit Manuel for the touchdown.

Now we're ahead by ten points, and I knew it was just about over. I mean, we weren't giving them shit. The wind was driving Schroeder crazy, just about shutting down their passing game, and we were taking care of the running. The wind kept bothering Schroeder, too. Late in the first quarter he had Gary Clark deep, alone, and the ball, which started out perfectly, suddenly got blown off to the side, and the guy had to stretch for it and dropped it at our 30. Even if he caught it and fell down right there it would have been a 33-yard gain. But he dropped it, and it was fourth down, so they punted. This time the ball went up and I swear it just hit a wall and fell down. It was a 24-yard kick.

Schroeder had just one more chance. Early in the second quarter, from their own four, their Pro Bowl wide receiver, Art Monk, got behind Elvis and caught a 48-yarder. Now they're on our 48, and we are going to have to fight them back. We wanted the shutout, see. It was starting to look possible and we really wanted it, kind of like the icing for our championship cake.

We held them. One more first down—barely—and Burt gets free in the middle and gets Rogers for a loss, and on third down Schroeder tries a pass and Perry Williams breaks it up. They've got no choice now, they have to get on the board, so in comes Jess Atkinson, who had kicked for us part of the previous season. He's gonna try a 51-yard field goal. But the snap was wild, Banks recovered the ball on the Redskins' 49 and from there we really put the game away.

I remember it was a second-and-15 situation on their 47. Simms goes to Bavaro again, down the left side. He beats linebacker Neal Olkewicz, makes the catch, and the free safety, Curtis Jordan, drags him down at the 16, a 31-yard gain.

Now the crowd is howling and screaming and the Redskins are starting to shrink, you know what I mean? They have taken so much, and nothing is working right for them. They're thinking about how their chance to get to the Super Bowl is getting smaller and smaller. Morris gained seven, Simms took the snap, rolled to his left and ran a naked bootleg down to the one-yard line. On the next play Joe went wide right. We had a 17-point lead.

I remember looking up at the clock. There was still 6:56 left to play in the first half, plus the entire second half, but I felt like the game was over. It wasn't that dangerous kind of cockiness; I could just feel it. We were playing so well, it almost seemed too easy. The Redskins had three more possessions in the half—they got no first downs, gained six yards total in all three chances and on fourth-and-one from our 28, with 54 seconds left, they went for it. George Rogers tried the middle, bounced off, went wide to his left, but Herb Welch and Pepper Johnson stood him up for no gain. That really was their last shot.

I think I'll remember the second half for a long time because almost everything the Redskins tried, we stopped. They were passing on almost every down by then. They ran a total of 37 plays in the second half and 34 of them were passes. Schroeder completed only 14. I got a long sack, 19 yards, about halfway through the third quarter, and that put them in such a deep hole that when they punted it was fourth-and-34 yards to go. In the fourth quarter Eric Dorsey nailed Schroeder, for another 19-yard sack. In the game we got him four times for 45 yards, and we kept their running game down to 40 yards total. It was a pretty good whipping all the way around.

Coach Gibbs and a lot of the Redskins said nice things about us afterwards—how we played so well, how the defense is impossible to come back against once we get a lead, how they thought we were the best team in the league and should be favored to win the Super Bowl. But then there was that Dexter Manley, the guy with the big mouth. Brad Benson had kept him harmless all game. Manley made only two tackles, didn't get near Simms, just didn't get much accomplished. But after the game he said that Benson was a good tackle but not a Pro Bowl guy, and that there were better tackles in the league. He also said he couldn't do the things he does best because the Redskins were behind. Well, that's true, but wasn't Dexter part of that defense that gave up the points that put them behind? I don't understand why he just wouldn't drop it and give Brad a little respect.

Now comes the best time, the most important thing from that game, maybe from the whole season—and that includes the Super Bowl.

It was almost eerie. When the game was over, everybody in the stadium stayed, stood up, and started yelling and screaming and making a strange kind of a howling noise. Nobody wanted to leave, they just wanted to stay and celebrate. Not many of them had seen the last Giant championship, which was way back in 1956. Hell, most of them probably weren't even born then.

Remember that wind? Well, it got stronger, and the fans started tearing up all kinds of paper, newspapers and programs and napkins and paper cups. Anything—ticket stubs, parking passes. They threw everything up in the air and the wind caught it and it swirled around and around the stadium. It was dark by then, one of those dark winter nights, the stadium lights were on and the paper formed little tornado-like funnels. The screaming went on and on as if it would never stop. It was just an unreal scene.

It was a celebration. It made us feel strange, like some great emotional thing was happening and it would be a once-in-a-lifetime experience. Then Jim Burt jumped into the stands and Pepper Johnson and William Roberts started doing a dance at midfield and, man, we all got into it. I had never experienced anything like that in my life, and I don't think I ever will again.

We did it! The Giants had made it to the Super Bowl. It was our eleventh straight victory, we had lost only two games since the season started way back in September, only once since the second week of the season, and now we were on our way to Pasadena. I had never played in the Rose Bowl before, and I couldn't think of a better way to start.

CHAPTER 13

"What do you guys know about football anyway?" **MEDIA MANIA**

There is a thin line between players cooperating with the sportswriters and the writers invading our privacy and writing things that can hurt the team and its morale. The problem exists in every pro sport. Sometimes there's a conflict when things aren't supposed to get out, are supposed to stay team business only, and somebody tells a writer or a writer overhears something, and suddenly the information is out and coach and the players get pissed.

The players are always trying not to say anything too juicy to the writers, and most of the guys understand that a writer covering the team is there to report the facts, on what's happening, what the coach and the players have to say and to describe the games that are played.

That's a reporter's job, and nobody will argue with anybody who writes the truth. But there is too much opinion mixed in, and frankly, there just aren't many sportswriters who understand the game the way we play it. That sounds snotty and I don't mean to be. I would never try to tell a writer how to write. But sometimes I think it's unfair that a sportswriter is expected to explain all kinds of stuff to his readers and he really isn't qualified to do that.

Now, the Giants' front office people are usually uncomfortable with the press. They want to maintain a certain kind of image and have things all their own way. Then the writers start to ask the wrong kind of questions and raise some doubts and get players talking about stuff they shouldn't be talking about. The Giants, probably more than any other team in the league, have more press people hanging around: fifteen, twenty guys on any given day, usually no less than nine or ten.

Since this is a tri-state area, we get daily reporters from the *Times, Daily News, Post, Newsday* from New York City. From New Jersey we get the *Star-Ledger, Bergen Record, Morristown Record, Paterson News, Passaic Herald-News* and *Asbury Park Press*. We get the *Hartford Courier, New Haven Journal and Courier* and *Bridgeport News* from Connecticut. Then there are other areas, like the Rockland–Westchester papers from New York, *USA Today*, sometimes occasional visits from papers in Boston, Rhode Island, Camden and Philadelphia. And that doesn't even count all the local radio stations and television stations. So you can see how many different guys we have to deal with. And women, too. It takes awhile to figure out which ones know what they're talking about and which ones are only looking for something controversial. It's a tough job, but I know it's part of the job so I try to be fair to everybody, answer all the questions but not be too open.

The team is concerned about image. They don't want to be perceived as a cheap, unprofessional organization anymore. They want to be seen as a strong, family-type organization, well established, fair-minded. They want to uphold that image.

Players are given advice on how to speak to the writers because a writer can ask a question and really be looking to trick you into saying something you shouldn't say or don't mean to say. The idea is not to say anything that won't sound right in the papers or on the air. It's the head coach who tells us how to handle the press. He talks to the players, says different things. You know, just don't ever overexpose yourself, don't give a guy anything important to write about you. I don't think he means for us to think of any writer as our enemy, but let's just say not exactly as our friend.

Their job is to write what they see, what they hear, what they see other people do, and that's something I've come to understand. Now, there's certain writers I just don't like. I read a story the other day in the *Giants' Newsweekly* about the defensive line. It was written by Hank Gola, who covers us regularly for the *New York Post*. It was talking about the defensive line position by position, and it sounded like he was going a little out of the way to be critical. Sometimes it's nice to write some things, but everybody doesn't always want to read negative shit. You get tired of reading all the negative stuff all the time.

Take the Sugar Ray Leonard fight with Marvin Hagler. I saw it. Sugar Ray fought the better fight, and people are still finding fault with him, saying he really didn't win. I guess there are guys who are disappointed we won the Super Bowl, too. I mean, if you're gonna write something negative, then you should write something positive, too. If you're gonna point out my weaknesses and shortcomings, then mention my assets, too, my strong points, the things I do best.

Bill never mentions specific writers, never. He's just very protective of the team, the players; he feels his obligation is to the players first, first and always. Lots of times the players talk about some of the writers, though. Some of them like certain guys and don't like others. Some of them don't like any of the writers and just won't talk. Zeke Mowatt is like that. Joe Morris, mostly. A few others. It took most of the season before Lawrence started talking to the writers. He would just shake his head and walk away when they tried to ask him questions. Mark Bavaro doesn't say anything, but he's just that way. He doesn't talk much to us, either. But in most of the cases, it's because a player was burned, said something to a writer that was supposed to be in confidence and then saw it in the paper, or said one thing and it was misunderstood or changed somehow and didn't mean the same thing.

See, the players have to deal with the press. Most of them don't much like it, but it's a fact of life. The reason is that the writers write such negative shit about them. Or they tell the truth, and sometimes players don't really like to see that, either. If they say somebody got beat on a pass that went for a touchdown, the player doesn't want to see his name in the paper, taking the blame for a loss.

They don't like a lot of the writers. I guess there are some sportswriters who don't do a good job, but they don't get cut. When a player doesn't do a good job, he gets cut. The press is supposed to report the best information, the factual information, and if they do, that's okay. But what makes it bad is all that negative stuff.

There's a built-in mistrust between players and the sportswriters. If a player has a bad game and a guy writes about it, then it's a problem and we can't solve it because that's the way it happened and it won't change. If a reporter says a guy dropped an easy pass in the end zone that would have been the winning touchdown and so the team lost, I guess that's negative. But it's also factual, reporting something just the way it happened. The radio and television people get us even worse sometimes, because our words are on their tape recorders and we can't deny saying something.

Parcells would rather we didn't say anything at all than take a chance of saying something that will hurt the team. He has to be that way. He's the head coach, and he is very much an experienced player's coach. There's another little problem, one that goes along with this media question.

The team president, Wellington Mara, has a lot of kids, and some of them work for the team. Two of them are Chris and Frank Mara, and they're usually hanging around the locker room, especially Frank. Chris is a scout, so I know what he does. But I'm not sure what Frank does, what his job description is, and I know he makes some of the players nervous. You know, they're afraid to do something, say something, because it might get back upstairs. I get along with everybody, just do my job and get the hell out, but it is an unusual situation, and it does make some players very uncomfortable.

Another thing about the press is how the newspapers built up that stuff about me in my rookie year, about how fat I was, how out of shape I was, what a stupid draft pick I was for the second round, really a weak draft choice, a player too short to play defensive end, too fat to play nose tackle, a player who wasn't figured to be a Pro Bowl player. Just didn't have a chance.

I've been able to give it all back to the critics, and sure, it bothered me to hear those things. But see, it was the truth. The reporters were just reporting the truth. I was a fat player. There was no way you could perceive a 290-pound defensive end who was out of shape to be an All-Pro player two out of the four years he's been playing. And I was only 6-3, and at least two or three inches shorter than most defensive ends today. I had the problems with my first marriage, all those other things, and now I've gone to be a better person, active in business, a community leader, the type of guy who has something to show for it, where he's come from, how far he's come. I never doubted my own abilities, but I was crushed because I had too many negatives working against me to really show what I had. That's what drove me to want to be a great ball player, to give it back to the critics, the skeptics. Today Ken and I sit and talk, and even he says that when we first met I was so screwed up I didn't know what was happening.

Things are really crazy at the Super Bowl. That whole week before the game the league tries to get all the publicity it can, so the teams must make the players available every day for a couple of hours. There must be two thousand media people, and they get fed breakfast or lunch and are taken to each team's training headquarters by chartered busses. The National Football League does everything possible to make things easy for the reporters, but really, they have to organize press conferences to do it that way because if you let two thousand guys loose in our hotel, there wouldn't be any way we could ever get any peace and quiet. At least this way it's organized; we know once the media time is over we can go back to practicing and relaxing and having our meetings with the coaches.

Another rule is that the players have to be cooperative. The people from the league make this very clear. We are all representatives of the league to the fans, and if there are people who want to ask us questions, we have to make ourselves available. So everybody agreed to cooperate, even the ones who seem press-shy. Lawrence, for one, said he'd talk on Wednesday, just Wednesday, and get everything answered so that he wouldn't have to show up for conferences the rest of the week. But he did. Zeke was talking to everybody, being polite and friendly. But he wouldn't say anything to the reporters who had regularly covered the Giants for two years. Somebody asked, why? He said because the league told him to. But usually he doesn't see any reason to talk to sportswriters because he thinks they just don't get things right.

The NFL designated Tuesday as Photo Day. That's when any photographer with an accredited pass, camera, videotape or anything else gets to meet us on the field where we practice, and we're supposed to pose for whatever shots they want. The writers show up at this thing, too. It's another chance for an interview, and I guess there's so much competition at the Super Bowl that they can't afford to be out sitting in the sun or lounging by the pool.

So a bunch of guys are there, waiting to talk to the players, and here comes Bavaro. They rush up to him and he just stares at them, kind of smiles a little smile, shakes his head and walks away. One of the writers runs after him and asks how come he's refusing to talk, since this is Super Bowl week and he's supposed to talk.

"This is Photo Day. I have to be here for photos. I don't have to talk today. I have to talk tomorrow." That's what he said, and even the writers got a laugh out of it.

CHAPTER 14

*"I guess I'd have to say
It was a lot better than
I thought it would be, and
a lot easier than I
thought, too."*

THE SUPER BOWL

We were the National Conference representative in the Super Bowl, and the week before we finally left for California was an absolute zoo. Seems like everybody I knew was calling for tickets, or just to say good luck, or to find out where we were going to stay so they could come visit. I just had to tell everybody that I had gotten enough tickets through the team to take care of my family, and there weren't any more and I wasn't going to start taking my mind off my job to scout up some more.

Coach Parcells was absolutely sensational in those first few days of preparation. He wanted to make sure that we didn't have anything to worry about except the game. He organized everything for us, from the way we'd be getting our tickets for family and friends to the hotel they'd stay in. He and the front office arranged for a chartered plane just for the families and office personnel. Transportation to their hotel was set up. It was all taken care of, so that we wouldn't be bothered.

Of course, we stayed in a separate hotel. That's league policy. But we stayed there only as long as the league insisted, and Friday morning before the game Parcells had arranged for us to spend the next day and a half in a kind of semi-isolation, away from the media and fans and even from our families and friends. People don't realize how time-consuming and annoying all those small personal details can become when players are trying to get ready for the biggest game of their lives.

I was surprised that so many Giant fans got tickets. They must have a lot more money than I ever thought, because when I looked up at the stands, especially in the second half, it seemed like everybody was wearing a blue sweater or a blue shirt and a blue hat, waving blue pennants and doing that "Go-o-o-o Giants" chant. My parents didn't go, they had something like a hundred people come to the house in Franklin. Everybody brought food and my father barbequed chicken and ribs. They watched the game on a big color television set and had a great time with all their friends and relatives. (My mother did come out to Hawaii, though, for the Pro Bowl the week after that. She went with Annette's parents and her uncle and three of her girlfriends.)

The fans were just unbelievable. Every day they were at our hotel, at the restaurants, just hoping to run into any of us. It was a nice feeling, you know? They were there for us, they were happy for us. One guy told me he had waited thirty years for this, that he loses sleep every time the Giants lose a game. Hey, Wellington Mara doesn't lose sleep over the Giants. These fans are something else. In a lot of ways it was like being home because everywhere we went, even in street clothes, there were people from New Jersey and New York who knew us, who were excited just to see us. It was a great atmosphere. It was like we took everybody from home and moved them to Southern California.

I must say I was savoring every minute of it. We never won a championship when I was in college, and now suddenly I'm in the middle of a Super Bowl setting and we're the favored team. We're playing a team we have already beaten, we're on that fantastic streak and we're coming off two playoff games where the combined score was 66–3. Just think about that for a minute. Sixty-six points were scored by our offense in two games against two of the better defensive teams in the National Football League. And against two great offensive teams like San Francisco and Washington, the Giant defense had allowed one damned field goal. And I don't think the Forty-Niners should have gotten that, either. Two shutouts would have been so nice.

I remember talking on the phone to my college coach, Pete Jenkins, and he kept telling me to just play my game. I talk to guys whose opinions I respect, like Ken, my father, Lamar, just to make sure I'm not getting into any bad habits. People who know about football can see something quick, before you're even aware of it. I was really excited about this game, about the hundreds of millions of people who would be watching us, about doing well and making people proud of the Giants. We all felt that way. We were determined not to make a single mistake, not to do anything wrong, not to say anything stupid to get the Broncos all riled up, not to stay out late, eat too much, drink too much. Nothing. We were going to come into that game sharp and hungry and mean. It meant too much to everybody, and nobody wanted to be the one to make something terrible happen.

Bill kept a tight check on us during the week. This had been our goal, and his, all year, and now that we were so close nobody was going to mess with it. We had regular bed check, just as we had had on road games during the season. We practiced hard because we had great respect for the Broncos, for John Elway, for their defense. We didn't fool around, crack too many jokes, stuff like that. We were a very serious bunch of guys that whole week, because we knew the celebrating could start as soon as we won the game. If we did something to cost us the game during the week, there'd be nothing but grief all winter.

I remember going out for dinner a couple of times during the week, but that was about it. Our days started real early, with mandatory breakfast, team meetings, the media sessions, then practice, then more meetings, dinner, a few hours on our own, more meetings and bed by eleven. Maybe everybody else was out there for fun in the sun, but we had to play the most important game the New York Giants had ever played. We wanted to come away with the trophy.

Remember when I said that my team as a kid was the Pittsburgh Steelers? Well, one reason was that they were tough, hard-nosed guys who came to the games to do an honest day's work. I respected that. But another reason was that they always won the big games. Always. They have been in four Super Bowls and their record is 4–0. That's what I want for the New York Giants, and that's what we all want. That is why we worked so hard that week, and why we were so serious.

During that week before the Super Bowl I spent a lot of time watching coach Parcells. I have to say that since we were rookies together in 1983—my first year as an NFL player, his first as an NFL head coach—he has become a totally different person. First, I have always been grateful to him because he drafted me in the second round that first year he was coach. And I was the first defensive lineman he had ever drafted, and knowing how much he knows about defense, that was a compliment, too. In a way, I was obliged to do well for him, to make him look good. But Bill was in his first year as a head coach and he had never been a proven head coach. He was hired in a quick decision by George Young when Ray Perkins suddenly resigned, and I think he was a young guy who just didn't have confidence either in himself or in other players. That led to a lot of problems we had. We had a lot of players who were going in different directions, trying to feel themselves out while the coach was learning, too.

Personality-wise, that team wasn't anything like this one. There were players with off-the-field problems. There were players who just weren't that good. We had a lot of guys suffer injuries that continued all season, guys who saw their careers end because of injuries. I think everybody knows that Bill came close to being a one-year coach, but that George decided one year under such circumstances wasn't a fair test. Does Bill make mistakes? Sure, he does. He's human, and every coach makes mistakes. He did a lot of things two, three years ago that he doesn't do now. I think he realizes he tried to get too close to the players in that first year. Sometimes that works if you have the right kind of player, but it didn't for him. He had to stay back, remain a little more distant.

Right after that Bill hired Johnny Parker, whom I had known when he was on the staff at LSU, to be our strength and conditioning coach. He has made such a difference. He has ideas on conditioning that are absolutely new to this sport. He has gone to the Soviet Union twice to learn their techniques and ideas. He designs a special program for every player, and his methods are so convincing that he has won over a lot of skeptics. Now, all year long there are guys in the weight room at six in the morning, lifting and working out and Johnny is always there, too, working with them. He has become one of my best personal friends, and I really think that Johnny Parker has helped the Giants become winners. Have you noticed how few injuries we have, and how we always seem to be at our best in the fourth quarter, especially in the last few minutes of a game? Credit Johnny, with his conditioning, stamina-building and endurance drilling. He has been as important to us as any coach on the field. I recommended him to Bill, told him that Parker would make people work. I told him that Johnny was going to do one of two things, either help these guys get better or prove that they weren't worth keeping. I know Johnny is very worried about L. T. now, because he doesn't spend much time in the weight room, doesn't seem to be interested in the program in the off-season.

When I first came up here, I was in awe of Lawrence and Harry, knew what great players they were and hoped that one day I'd be able to start on the same defense with them. Now we've all made the Pro Bowl the past two years, and in my case I have to thank Johnny Parker for a lot of it. He is my "body manager" just like Ken Wirth is my money manager. Johnny tells me if I stay loyal to the system, if I stay in shape, that I can be a consistent twelve-to-fifteen-sack player every year. I intend to do everything possible, because this is my life and my income and I'm not nearly finished playing yet. There are more Super Bowls to win.

I'm not content yet. There are things I want to do. I know I can get better. I'd like to play six more years, and then retire. George Martin told people that last year was going to be his final one, that he was going to retire— especially if we won the Super Bowl—and now he's coming back anyway. I guess it's tough to leave. It'll probably be tough for me, too.

Finally, it was game day. Super Sunday. It was a very quiet team bus, everybody thinking his own thoughts, making sure of assignments, concentrating on the guy he had to go up against for the biggest prize in pro football. It's usually quiet before a game, but this time it was even more so. I don't think we were as much afraid of the Broncos as we were just uptight and nervous. How else can you feel when you're this close to the Super Bowl? It's something you've dreamed about for years and the closest you ever got to it is the front of your television set.

Fittingly, we played a super game. Defensively, I think we played the best, or close to the best, that we had played all year. At times during the game, those tunes came to me again, running around my head. I remember one that was a jazz tune, by Wynton Marsalis. It's not unusual, as I've said, but this was the Super Bowl.

You know what made us feel good about the game? We were trailing at halftime, 10–9, and yet we felt really good because the Broncos had played their best half of the season, doing almost everything right, and they were only winning by one point. We had played pretty badly, letting their offense get away with too many things. And still all they were ahead was just one point.

Right near the end of the first half, two things happened that made the Broncos realize what the second half was going to be like. They had already missed one field goal, a chip shot from 23 yards away. On the first play of their next series, I beat my guy and dropped Elway on the 13 for a two-yard loss. Now it's third-and-12, Elway drops back to pass, I'm putting pressure on (getting held, of course) and George comes in from the other side and nails him in the end zone. I mean, just blows by the guys trying to block him and drops Elway for a safety. So, on a three-play series the Elway kid gets sacked once by me and two plays later gets sacked—for a safety—by George.

Now he's starting to get a little nervous. They get the ball back and he can't accomplish anything. Their kicker misses another field goal and the half ends. We had good reason to walk off confidently, even though we were trailing, because we had just taken the best they could do and we kicked most of it back in their faces.

That second and third quarter were the two best our defense played all season. I thought Carl Banks and I played the best any two defensive players had played in that game. Somebody said that there was some sentiment to make me the Most Valuable Player, but Phil Simms was just magnificent. There was no other choice but him. And if I had been asked, I'd have said that after Phil, Carl Banks should have been given the consideration. He had a great, great game. He had ten unassisted tackles, covered on passes, made people change their plays, got double-teamed. I played good, I really did, and when I think how close I came to two more sacks—right in a row early in the second quarter—I still get upset. It was their first series of the quarter, and on a second-and-12 I got close, but he just got the ball away and was incomplete. Then on the very next play I just missed him. I had my fingers on his jersey, and he flipped the ball away and it turned into a 54-yard completion, down to our 28. And their kicker missed that 23-yard field goal.

When we came out for the second half, the moment of truth was at hand. We used another fourth-down call to get a first down when we shifted once the signals were called and put Jeff Rutledge in a quarterback position. When he took the snap he just ran the middle. He got two yards. We only needed one. Then Simms started hitting all those passes, 12 yards to Morris, 23 to Lee Rouson and finally 13 to Bavaro for the touchdown. It was our first lead since early in the first quarter, and the last time the Broncos were close enough to even think about taking it back.

They took the ball, ran three plays, gained five yards and punted. We scored with a field goal. They took the ball again, ran three more plays, punted and we scored, a touchdown run by Morris for one yard after a 44-yard flea-flicker play from Simms to McConkey down to the one. Remember that? Poor Phil was tackled at the one, didn't get the touchdown and just threw himself on the ground, moaning.

The quarter was nearly over. Denver got the ball once

more in the period—and I sacked Elway again, an 11-yarder, my second of the game. Two plays later, in the fourth quarter, Patterson intercepts him—by now Elway is really pressing—and we score again. McConkey finally got his touchdown when he pulled down a ball that had bounced off Bavaro's hands. We were all glad for him, all celebrating on the sidelines. That gave us a 33–10 lead.

We started celebrating then, because there was no way they were going to get close. We even got another touchdown late, when Phil kept the ball on a third-and-six and ran for 22 yards to the Broncos' two-yard line. Then Bill did a nice thing. He brought in Ottis Anderson, who's been in the league a long time and has had a great career, and gave him the chance to score a touchdown in the Super Bowl. He did, slamming over right up the middle.

It got a little weepy then, you know. All those fans in the stands, and I swear they were all the people from Giants Stadium, started screaming and standing up. Then the public address system in the Rose Bowl starts playing that Sinatra song, "New York, New York," and everybody starts singing along, yelling out the words, and it was like our own personal party, you know? I guess the Broncos really felt lousy right about then, because we had beat them every which way. We had held them to 52 yards rushing—Elway had 27 of them—and sacked their quarterback and kept him down and he is supposed to be the best in the league.

I remember after we beat Washington, somebody asked John Madden what he thought Elway would do. He said he didn't think Elway would do anything because the Giants had as much speed on the ends of their defense, the outside linebackers, as Elway had, except the Giant guys were 50 pounds heavier. They could catch him, not just chase him, and when they did he was going to feel it. And he said the linebackers would keep him from scrambling much, would force him back to the inside. It all worked out just that way. I don't think Elway really could have hurt us that day, not unless he got off a few lucky passes.

We were Super Bowl champions, and for millions of people it was the end of a dream. Like Parcells said, now that the Giants have finally won the championship, all the ghosts can be buried. The ghosts with names like Tittle, Conerly, Robustelli, Huff, Gifford, Rote and all the rest. The New York Giants are Super Bowl champions. These New York Giants. I'm thankful for all the love these guys have shown me, and I admire the way they've set a standard for today and for future generations of Giants. I'm honored to be a part of it all.

CHAPTER 15

"I don't think I could live in Franklin now, the pace is just too slow. But the people are great and every time I go home there are great memories . . . except, I guess, when I think about what happened to some of my closest boyhood friends."

FRANKLIN, LOUISIANA

Franklin is about a hundred and ten miles from New Orleans, a hundred miles from Baton Rouge. It's where I grew up, my hometown, where I was a poor black kid, a country black kid in the Deep South. What were my chances?

My father, Leonard Marshall, didn't make enough money, even though he worked at two different jobs, to support my mother and the kids. For almost all of my childhood years I never saw much of him on any given day. See, one job he'd work from seven in the morning to three or four in the afternoon as a shipbuilder, a carpenter, come home for an hour, eat something, shower and shave, and then go work in a bar until midnight. Then he'd get up at five the next morning, catch a van and go to work from seven to three. He did that for fourteen years. But things have got real bad down there now, with the oil business falling apart, and over the past two years I don't think he's made more than $20,000 total. There's hardly any work back home for anybody these days. Sure, I help, of course I do. It's my honor and my privilege, after all the things he did for me.

But if I grew up poor, I surely didn't grow up unhappy. First of all, Franklin is a predominantly black town, and since most of my friends were black and we were all basically in the same situation, we didn't really know we were poor. It wasn't until we started getting bussed to a white school that I realized we didn't have much. We were wearing old clothes and riding old bicycles, and a lot of the white kids had all new clothes, expensive bikes, stuff like that. I started to see there was a difference. Until I was six years old I had gone to a predominantly black Catholic school, and then I was transferred to a predominantly white school, even though it was integrated. They had a quota of black kids they had to accept. It was a public school, but my first one was private, until I reached the third grade.

I didn't have much trouble. I was always big as a kid and I guess nobody really wanted to fool with me. My father's a short guy, about 5–10, but so strong. My mother is six feet tall, but my father's father was 6–7 and 360 pounds. So I get my size from both sides of the family. I remember playing Biddie Basketball—we had the best team in the state that year—and we had the chance to play in the national tournament if we won one more game. But then, well, there was a rule that any kid over 5–7½ wouldn't be eligible. And when they checked my height, they found I was 5–8. So I had to sit out, and that made me feel different, self-conscious, I guess. That doesn't happen to me anymore. I know I'm a big man and I like it. Other people look up to me, care about what I say and do. But when you're a kid, that kind of thing can make you feel funny, like a freak. And then when I went out for football they told me I couldn't play, I was too big and too heavy. At the age of twelve, I was 5–8 and I weighed 145 pounds, and they wouldn't let me play Pee Wee Football. I was a good basketball player, really good, and I honestly didn't know which sport I loved more, basketball or football.

In my junior year in high school, the football coach told me it was time to make a choice, and he told me to pick football. "Son," he said, "you're gonna be so big, so strong, you're already so fast, I want you to play linebacker. Basketball isn't your sport, you like to run into too many people."

So I stayed in his football program, and I went from 205 pounds one spring to 230, lifting weights and eating a lot of peanut butter. I got real strong real fast. I started, we went to the district championship but lost that game. In my senior year we didn't have a good team but I played linebacker, defensive tackle and offensive tackle, and I played very well. I also had my weight up to 245 by then, and there was a lot more muscle than fat. Then I made my choice between different scholarship offers, and I was up to 250 when I went to LSU as an incoming freshman.

I have picked up a lot of common sense from the streets, from growing up where I did, how I did. I learned from other people's mistakes, too, and when I see them make a mistake I try to remember it so I won't do the same thing. I've had to teach myself about money, and I've had to learn which people are looking to grab some of it. Hey, I've got a relative who's been after me for years, wanting to start a restaurant in Texas. I just don't think it'll work, and I know he's angry with me for not just giving him the money. I've had people approach me, but I usually push them aside. If they can show me the numbers, the deals, tell me about other people who have joined, their names, how they made out, then I'll consider it. But I know an athlete who makes a lot of money is a target for a lot of those people, and I don't mean to let them take me for a ride.

I loved growing up in Franklin. I think part of the reason for going to LSU was to stay close to home, to be with my family, to watch my six brothers and sisters grow up, too, and to be there for them if they needed or wanted any help. I think being close to home also kept me out of trouble during my college years. I mean, I wasn't a troublemaker, but who knows what would have happened if I was two thousand miles away. I always wanted to play for my home state, too, and this made it possible. I was recruited by a lot of schools, and I guess Oklahoma would have been my second choice, but I have never regretted picking LSU.

There was a lot of money in Franklin, but it was old money. There were white people who still lived there whose families had been wealthy for a hundred years. It was old money handed down generation to generation, and there were black families like that, too. Now all the blacks in the South, in Louisiana, are poor. It was never as if a young guy could go out, start a business, make a lot of money and get rich. It still doesn't work like that for the blacks.

The blacks who have money have always had it, or have had it for a long, long time. There's only two or three black guys now who made it all on their own, who just worked so damned hard that it happened for them, and I'm very proud of those people. The whole South has had racial trouble, but Franklin isn't the kind of town where things were really Klannish, so to speak. Between 1972 and 1973, racial protest broke out, but I was in elementary school. I didn't really take much part in it.

I graduated from high school when I was barely seventeen. I liked school, and whatever else I was doing I always managed to keep my grades high. I knew even then, I guess, that if I was going to make anything happen for myself, it was going to be through getting a college education.

My parents were poor and black, but there are millions of people who are poor and white. No big thing. We all know where we came from, what we had and what we didn't have. When the town had a Leonard Marshall Day last February, black people and white people came out. It was really important and satisfying to me. I am the first football player who ever came from Franklin and played on a Super Bowl championship team. When I took Annette with me, there was no problem. The blacks treated her with great respect, and the whites treated me with the same respect. I know, people are going to say it's because I'm a pro athlete, a Super Bowl athlete, that they're nice to me. But they were that way before, too. I don't think Franklin has any racial problem now. People there understand each other. Franklin is an older town, and we had all our black–white bullshit a hundred years ago. Things changed a long time ago for the better, so now we just accept each other. There is no white trash in Franklin, no black trash either.

I had a lot of friends in Franklin and still do, but some of those guys I was really friendly with have gone in the wrong direction. They have allowed bad things, bad people, to pull them into trouble, into failure, and they were athletes just as good as me or better, who could have gotten out through sports.

I grew up with some pretty wild guys. For example, one of the guys could have been one of the best small forwards in the NBA right now. He could have been rolling in cash, just like Clyde Drexler—he's in the NBA now, and he's from Franklin, too. This kid, who happens to be an old friend, went to the state penitentiary for sixty dollars.

Armed robbery. For sixty bucks. Robbed an old man who couldn't hear. Held him up at gunpoint. He didn't need the money, either. But I loved him like a brother, and I'm still in touch with his family.

There are only three guys there whom I grew up with and were my best friends, the only three I was so close to we were really like brothers, family, blood.

One of them was Lyman White, who was with the Atlanta Falcons for a while. He was a linebacker and one day he injured his knee and they found a tumor in his leg. So they could no longer keep him because he could no longer play football after that kind of surgery. For a long time, he was doing well, then I heard he was struggling, and I was trying to put together a dinner for him. I wanted to do something right, but when I tried to hook it up, things just wouldn't come together. I couldn't get people to cooperate. But he's back on his feet now, he came through it safely and I heard he opened a restaurant. He lost his father right before he found out he had cancer; his father got stabbed to death. A lot of bad things happened to him at a young age, but Lyman was always strong, always ready to fight back, and I think finally things are working out for him.

The next guy, Michael Ray, was another great athlete when we were in high school, a guy I thought was going to become a major league baseball player. The guy had a lot of talent, but just didn't make it. He still lives in Franklin.

The third guy, Jerry Hall, was a good athlete who had the chance to do something for himself, but he just didn't have anything to drive him. It was like his life was built around parties, being a dude, a street guy, being involved with the action. He had nothing to motivate him, to push him. I don't know what he's doing now. I don't know if he's alive or dead.

I don't hear from those guys anymore, and that bothers me. Oh, I've talked to Lyman a few times, but it isn't the same, you know? When they held Leonard Marshall Day in Franklin, my family really had the chance to enjoy that, to really, really feel the success I've had. And they know the struggle I went through to make it to where I am now. They love me for it, the whole town is proud of me and that makes me feel so proud I can't describe the feeling. One thing really hurt me, though. I was told that Lyman's mom felt that she couldn't attend that day, didn't want to, because they had never done anything like that for her son when he made it with the Falcons. He had made it to the NFL, and the townspeople never felt they should have a day to show how proud they were of him and his family, the way they did for me and for my family.

See, the thing she had to remember is that we're all one family down there, and that I had accomplished something that nobody from Franklin had ever accomplished before, playing on a world championship football team and being in the two Pro Bowl games either, right? Somebody from Franklin may not do that for another twenty years, and if he does, then they should have a day for him, too. And not too many people from that area can say they made the kind of money I'm making, gotten the kind of exposure I've gotten, accomplished all the things I've accomplished at such a young age.

What drove me? Watching pro football on television as a kid and knowing that's what I wanted to do. We were all the same age, and I just wanted to be someone, wanted to do something. Also, I was moved by the way my father was always working, always doing anything he could for his family, to pay our bills, to put food on our table. I used to tell him, "Hey, daddy, you're not gonna see me hanging around the barroom where you work, ordering drinks from you. I'm gonna make you proud of me, do something with my life."

When it came time for me to go to college, he was really proud; he knew I was going to do something good. He told his friends that they'd all hear about his son before too long. And I've always hoped my brothers and sisters would pick up where I left off, doing things that are important. Now one of the girls is about to finish music school, and another of the boys, Chris, is going to become a pro next year—he's playing at Tulane now—and he's going to be drafted as a linebacker. The baby, Kenneth, is about to go off to college and he may have the success that we hoped to have but didn't. It's good. My father tried to come to my games at LSU when he could, but he was usually working. My mother couldn't drive, so she couldn't go. Also, she never wanted me to play football, she was afraid for me. She said you're never too big to get hurt. She wanted me to just go to school and become a professional, like a doctor or a lawyer. Both my parents have always been strong on college. Neither of them ever graduated from high school, but knew that if they had, their lives would have been better, with more opportunities.

I guess that's about all there is. I wanted to write this book more to make a statement, to tell people what I'm about, who I am, the things I stand for and some things I'll never stand for. I know I'm only twenty-six years old: who am I to write a book about myself? But I'll tell you this. I'm more than just a professional football player. I want people to like me for who I am, not what I am.

Now I live in a quiet neighborhood in northern New Jersey. My neighbor is an Indian doctor, and there is a good mix of other nationalities in the town. We talk to each other, see each other in our houses, make friends. We don't care about color or religion. I don't care if the guy next door is a doctor, and my neighbors don't care that I'm a football player.

That's how it should be. You know I never think of

myself as black anymore. I just think of myself as Leonard, married to Annette, friendly to anybody who wants to be my friend. I don't like labels or tags, and I never put them on other people. I just wish they wouldn't put them on me.

CHAPTER 16

"What's a nice Italian girl like you...?" **ANNETTE**

Annette DiNapoli Marshall, twenty-two years old, is my wife. She was born and raised in a deeply rooted Italian–American area in Jersey City, New Jersey, and she'll admit, now, that her father, Gaetano, was a bit over-protective. But we have to say "was," because after Gaetano's little girl married this great big black guy who was born in rural Louisiana and weighs nearly 300 pounds, I think Gaetano DiNapoli came to love me not like a son-in-law but like a son.

I think if I had made that statement six months ago, and if Gaetano DiNapoli heard me talk like that and found out I was going to marry his daughter, I might have had a midnight visit from guys named Guido and Aldo. After all, she's a full-blooded Ne-apo-li-tan.

Annette doesn't laugh. "Did I ever think I'd wind up marrying a black guy? God, no. To be honest, that kind of thought would never have entered my mind. As I got older, I dated all kinds of guys. But marry Leonard? No way." Now she laughs.

Annette DiNapoli became Mrs. Leonard Marshall on Sunday, April 5, 1987, in one of the most elegant catering halls in New Jersey. We were not allowed to marry in church—at least, Catholic Annette wasn't—because my previous marriage had ended in divorce rather than by annulment.

"I would have liked a church wedding," she says, shrugging her shoulders, "but I love him, so what difference does it make?"

Annette is of medium height, around 5–5 with a trim figure (despite her complaint that she's put on twenty pounds since she moved in with Leonard), striking black eyes, shoulder-length black, glossy hair, a bright, bubbly personality that lights up a room and a quick sense of humor.

"It was a little difficult at first," she says, "especially with my father. He wasn't that thrilled about Leonard being black, but I think he was bothered even more by the fact that Leonard was a professional football player. Oh, he had this idea that Leonard was just interested in using me, taking advantage of me and then throwing me aside, and he didn't want that to happen to his little girl. So it got pretty tense in my house for a while."

In fact, Annette left home for a while, lived with a girlfriend, and then, after we had talked for weeks, I figured it was time for her to move in with me, that it would be the best thing for both of us to really get an idea of whether it was going to work. So she did, and that was the end of it. Or I should say, that was the beginning of it.

The DiNapoli family relented. And why not? After all, *they* didn't have to feed me.

"Sure, I brought him back home. I'm Italian. I might have left the house, but the family is always there. Of course I kept going back—I just didn't live there, that's all. Anyway, once I started showing up with Leonard, and my father got to know him, it all changed. Now? God, I hate it when they're together. They get off by themselves and all they do is talk football and finances and they are both boring. I mean, really boring.

For a while it was a lot like *Guess Who's Coming to Dinner?* But then things cooled off. Now there's no problem at all. I don't think there ever really was one, just something new that older people had to have time to think about and adjust to. My family, also. They never thought that I'd wind up marrying an Italian. Neither did I.

We met at a cocktail party in 1984 for a bunch of legal people in Hudson County, and she didn't give me the time of day. A bunch of lawyers, prosecutors and police officers were there, and Annette came along with one of her girlfriends. She worked for the Hudson County prosecutor's office. She was being a snob, but I think she was just playing hard to get. She didn't even want to talk to me. I didn't know if it was because I was black, or a football player, or because I was too damned big, or what.

I was told she was engaged. Well, I didn't want to deal with that because I figured if she was engaged, she was happy and I wouldn't have a chance, you know? But she wasn't really engaged. Just having a good time but not really happy with what she had. Finally, she agreed to go out with me, and after we started truly dating, I started to see something in her that I had never seen in any other girl. I think, now that I know her, that it was her strong will, her determination not to make things appear different. Underneath all that Italian pastry is a tough, streetwise lady, devoted, good and, in the truest sense of the words, color-blind.

There has never been any trouble with my family or my friends, once everybody saw this was serious. That goes for Annette's people, too. No problems in public either. And since we intend to stay with the same people in the same area, I don't expect any.

Of course, there were all those whispers that Annette was marrying me because I earn $500,000 a year and because I have started to put in place a network of real estate holdings that will secure our financial comfort for the rest of our lives. Marrying me for my money? Wrong. So much for the whispers.

What about the pressures that a mixed marriage can create? None. I don't think we have taken on any additional grief. It draws us closer actually, makes us more grateful for what we have. A lot of people may see it as black and white, but I know a lot of guys who are involved in mixed marriages. My family and Annette's family have come to respect and love one another and, you know, they have a lot in common. Her father and my father both worked very hard all their lives, stayed with their families and brought up the kids right. They were poor all their lives, they know where they come from. It's not like they're a snooty white upper-class family, or that we're a snooty black upper-class family. We all know what it's going to take to make our lives together more fruitful.

Annette has visited my family in Franklin several times, went with me in February when the town celebrated Leonard Marshall Day in honor of the Super Bowl victory with a parade and dinner, and not once was she made to feel uncomfortable. Hell, some of the people thought she was just a light-skinned black. I don't think I'd want to live in Franklin again, but if I did, we could do it without being bothered. There are other interracial couples there. Oh, I suppose some people would try to make us feel uncomfortable, not necessarily in Franklin, but anywhere.

The hometown people showed nothing but respect for Annette. She met a lot of my friends, and they showed her a good time. See, we have no problem, have faced no problem. We never have a situation of not being able to check into a hotel. But that doesn't mean there isn't any problem in Louisiana. Man, there are towns in Lousianna that black people aren't allowed in. Towns like Lafitte, and Pierre Part where lower-class, ignorant whites still think they're better than average whites and blacks.

People wonder how my teammates, from whom I want friendship and respect, have behaved now that I have an Italian wife. Nobody has ever said anything mean or nasty. They do joke about it, though. There are a lot of black players on our team involved with white women. I'd say at least twenty percent of them have white wives or girlfriends. Also, I have a lot of black and Hispanic friends who date white girls or who have married white girls. And I know white guys who either have black fiancees or black wives. It's really not important anymore. Society, around here anyway, accepts people for what they are, who they are. Mostly who they are, I think.

Malcolm X had a lot of interesting things to say, and some historians think Malcolm was more influential among younger blacks than Dr. King. I studied Black History all through the Sixties. As a kid I always wore the black power colors, the black, red and green. I followed the Black Panthers, I was really into reading about it. It was something I chose to do, it didn't matter what anybody else felt. But it was wrong, I realized, and I felt I couldn't support the Panthers. The militant attitude wasn't my attitude. I felt I should be courteous to white people, and attempt to deal with everyone differently. Blacks perceived white people as dogs, not to be associated with, tried to teach young blacks to be strong in the quest of their goals. It was my idea to live on both levels, to deal with all people, no matter what their color. Hey, there are black guys I really dislike as well; white guys, too. I never hated white people when I was growing up. I envied what they had, maybe, but I didn't hate them.

There are people here who don't care for blacks. Yet in my neighborhood, there are all kinds of ethnics on the the block. These are expensive houses, a good neighborhood. There are Jewish families, an Indian family, Italians. People who are independent and very successful businessmen, and we all get along. I'm the guy who walks around the neighborhood with a basketball, shooting at other people's baskets. Children of the neighbors bring their friends around to meet me, to get my autograph. I'm happy to do that, it's fun. I think I get along because I don't carry on about being this big successful jock, you know? I'm just Leonard who takes care of his lawn and washes his car in the driveway. To a lot of the kids in the neighborhood I'm just plain Mr. Marshall. There are people everywhere who have problems dealing with blacks, including them, not really able to see the person because skin color is blinding them. So what? But Malcolm X had a message, and under all his militancy he was a logical man. He said that by the year 2000 everybody would be coffee-colored. It won't happen, but I like the concept. It's beginning to matter less and less what people think about color in most places of the world. Annette and I never think about it anymore, not unless somebody else mentions it.

Money, you know, is the great equalizer. It's amazing how quickly bigoted white people suddenly accept blacks, as when Wilt Chamberlain built his million-dollar house in Bel Air, California. He wasn't a black anymore, just the tall gentleman who lives on the hill.

I believe the militant age is over. Blacks and whites are going to be on equal grounds, maybe they are already. Things are getting better all over. I remember when we went to Atlanta once, I got in a cab to go to dinner. The cab driver, a white guy, said, "Hey, brother"—that was the first time I ever had a white call me brother, by the way. "Hey, brother, about ten miles from here is Cummings, Georgia, and don't you go there. Blacks ain't allowed there after six o'clock. The story is they hung a black man there for having sex with a white woman years ago."

It's only in the poor areas, the poor-trash areas, where this is still prevalent, where people's minds are warped with the idea of dealing with one another, black on white, white on black. I just don't understand. What difference does it make if I'm black and you're white, if one guy is Puerto Rican and another guy is Jewish? Did it ever make any difference? I don't think so. I really don't think so.

I remember a trip to a synagogue in New Jersey, where I was invited to speak. It was called Temple Israel, and there were kids and their fathers and everybody was white. And Jewish. And the kids all had clippings of stories about me from magazines and newspapers, and they wanted me to autograph them and they were truly friendly. They didn't care that I was black. I think after we talked for a while, most of them probably didn't consciously remember I was black. We were just a bunch of guys talking sports, talking football. Not white guys, not black guys, just guys. Talking sports and at the same time showing God that it didn't matter what color we were. I think that was important; it showed everybody what the world could be like if people just drop all that stuff about color.

There are no black head coaches in the National Football League, and never have been. It is becoming more and more a cause for black leaders, but there should be black head coaches only if they're qualified. There probably are a lot of black guys who are qualified, but I don't think it's necessarily racism if they're not hired. It could be a disbelief that black men can lead an organization; it could be the owners don't really believe that a black guy could lead a team to a championship. I think that once a guy puts his foot in the door and proves that a black guy can be as good a head coach as a white guy in the league, then it'll spread. I don't think there's a plot to keep black men out of head coaching jobs. I just think the owners don't feel they're ready to make that kind of decision.

But I sure as hell don't want a black man to get a head coaching job just because he's black. That's bullshit, and that can be damaging in the end. Same thing with black quarterbacks, which there have been. In the beginning the stereotype thinking prevailed. People in charge would say, "Hey, they can't play quarterback, they can't remember plays, they're not smart enough." That was racism, but now it's just a lack of development at those positions. You know, white quarterbacks make mistakes, too; they just never had to carry the stigma through life that they weren't mentally qualified. But colleges don't recruit black quarterbacks, so they go to small schools and don't get the same coaching and chances. I've seen a lot of black quarterbacks who played well but never got a chance (in the NFL). I can't understand it, I wish I knew whether it's racism or disbelief. But look, we've had Doug Williams, Matthew Reed, James Harris, Joe Gilliam, and Vince Evans. There are black quarterbacks on current rosters, such as Warren Moon, Reggie Collier, Randall Cunningham. For years there were no black centers, and it couldn't make any difference what color the centers were, that was just the way it was. Look, I don't want the reputation of a guy who's always crying about racism and injustice. I know it exists. I also know there are things that are just the way they are and won't be changed unless something happens and it has nothing to do with racism or prejudice. I'm a black guy, but I'm not going to say black is always better than white just because I'm black.

For that matter, I'm not going to say men are always better than women just because I'm a man. Right, Annette?

Annette: "Right."

As you can see, nobody has the last word in this marriage. Right, Annette?

Annette: "Right."

CHAPTER 17

"We showed a lot of character, a lot of camaraderie, a lot of love for each other, and I have to give most of the credit to Bill Parcells."

BILL PARCELLS

The key to our success last year, the instrumental leader, was Bill Parcells. He kept a level head, kept us calm, under control, wouldn't even let us celebrate the victories as we got closer to the championship. He made sure to bring us back down to earth after each win. I didn't realize then just how much of a settling influence he really was. He'd harp on some mistake that really wasn't so important, or he'd find a different thing entirely to bitch about to us: blame the press for writing something, tell us what some Redskin said, what some Cowboy said—all of this designed to just keep our feet on the ground and prevent us from getting cocky.

For a guy only four years on the job, it's amazing how good a job he did keeping us focused on the important things and developing young talent. He has continued to grow as a head coach, and his players have grown with him. I think this Giant team is going to be strong for a long time, and I don't think we'd be nearly as good, or as confident, without Bill as our coach.

In the beginning, if you hadn't known Bill Parcells, I

guess you would have categorized him as a blue-collar worker who was constantly worried about losing his job. It's like a situation in a factory. Somebody's the boss, in this case Bill, and you're his slave, and if you abide by the rules you'll come to be a good worker. By virtue of that, he has developed a lot of young guys into great players.

He treats all the players a little differently. He seems to know what each player needs and how each guy has to be treated in order to get him to play as hard as he can. In the beginning he was a little rough on me because he knew the ability I had, he knew the guy I worked for in college—Pete Jenkins, my line coach. Pete, Lamar Leachman and a whole bunch of those guys all worked together down at South Carolina, so Bill knew about me from Pete and Lamar. He knew a lot more about me, I guess, than most other coaches in the league. Before I was drafted, they talked a lot and Bill knew he wanted a raw talent like myself; for me to play that position if not the first year then the second for sure. I knew he had been having some problems with Gary Jeter at right end, and when he decided to trade him, he knew he had to have somebody new at that position, some young guy with potential to fill the role.

He has helped me grow as a player and as a person. His complaint about me showing up overweight was blown out of proportion. Sure, I was overweight, eight or ten pounds over the weight I was supposed to be. The real problem was my condition. But Bill made a point of making fun of me, of telling the writers how fat I was. You know, they were making up those jokes, "How fat is he?" It took a lot for me to respond positively to all that pressure, and I thank Bill Parcells for making me the kind of player I am today. He never let up. I remember once, during that summer of my rookie season, thinking about resigning and going back to Louisiana. Maybe this football deal just wasn't for me. But you know what? Thinking about having to tell Bill just flat changed my mind. He had put a lot of faith in me, a lot of trust. He had taken me high in the second round, and whether or not I should have been a first-round pick—and I should have—he showed enough confidence in me to do it. I was the thirty-seventh player in the country to be drafted, and when you think about that, it's pretty high, it's a nice compliment. I was his guy, the defensive lineman he really wanted, the highest drafted defensive lineman the Giants had taken since 1976, when they took Troy Archer in the first round.

That's a guy I would like to have played with. Everybody says he would have been the absolutely perfect nose tackle, a guy 6–4 and 270, strong as a bull, just wanted to play defense. A quick guy who played mean. He played three years, started all three of them as a defensive tackle, and just when he was coming into his Pro Bowl stage as a player he was killed when his van went out of control on a wet road in the rain. It happened the summer that Ray Perkins and George Young had been hired, and it sure was a major blow to their defensive plans for that first season. The next year, when Perkins changed the defense into a 3–4, Archer would have definitely been his nose tackle.

But Parcells wanted me, and what did I do to show him how grateful I was? I showed up overweight and out of condition. So it was my obligation to show him I was worthwhile, that he didn't make a mistake. That's why, that one time when I considered scrapping all the crap and just walking out, I couldn't do it. Man, am I glad I didn't.

We get along great, but the one thing I don't really like about him, the only thing really, is that sometimes we'll be talking and I just can't get him to answer me straight. Sometimes he just goes around and around, not wanting to give me an answer. Like when we talk about money or contracts. He just doesn't like to get involved in player stuff. We'll talk in circles and just can't come to an agreement. That's the thing I don't like the most. I don't like it when you're having an open discussion with people, trying to be real with them, and they aren't helping. Hey, that's the kind of person I am. Just say what you have to say, say it out loud and direct, and let me deal with it. I'm that way, my friends are mostly that way. If Bill was a little more like that, I think our relationship would be better.

But as a player–coach relationship there is no problem at all. That man is an excellent, outstanding defensive coach. Shit, President Reagan should hire him, make him Secretary of Defense. Put him up there and let him be the man to fire those damned missiles.

There are certain things that Bill really thinks are important. For example, we go to a hotel in Woodcliff Lake, New Jersey, the night before home games. Man, it's crazy there, but Bill thinks it's important for us to be together the night before a game, just as we are on the road. There are kids there mobbing the players, mobbing the lobby. A lot of the guys just lay around in their damned rooms, you know, trying to avoid being bothered. Others are trying to sneak out of the hotel and go back home. I've tried it a few times myself, but then I think about getting caught and it deters me from leaving. Bill makes it mandatory, which means there is a fine. So we don't do it. Or most of us, anyway, don't do it.

I remember a funny incident one night at summer camp. First you have to remember that Bill is very particular about keeping bed check and curfew during summer camp. Well, a bunch of guys, including Lawrence Taylor, snuck out after eleven, to go to town for a few beers, but L. T. was the only one who got caught. And he swears he got caught because Johnny Parker was hiding in the bushes, watching for players leaving. Was Johnny hiding in the bushes? I don't know, but if he was, I'm sure Parcells put him up to it.

The best thing Bill Parcells does is make the players feel like he's always thinking about what's best for them. He protects us from the media, from management, from those outside people who always seem to be hanging around the team. You know, there are a lot of people who work with the team, who travel with the team, who are always asking us to do something. Bill calls them the E.R.W.'s of the team: They Eat, Ride and Warm up with the Giants. It's pretty obvious he doesn't think much of people who are trying to distract the players, but most of them are involved with the ownership, so what can you do about them? They're just there.

Right after the Super Bowl, there was a story that Bill's agent, Robert Fraley, had asked for permission for Bill to talk to the Atlanta Falcons about their head coaching job, but the Giants refused. Well, I'm not so sure how serious it really was. It seemed like his agent was doing all the talking, maybe using it as a bargaining thing. If he's like Ken Wirth, I know he was doing that. Hey, Bill should get a new contract, he deserves a lot more money. They're gonna tear up his old contract and give him a new one. They should. But I don't think he was really serious about Atlanta. It's a nice enough place and all, but this is where Bill belongs, right here in New Jersey, where he's from. He loves this part of the country, the people. They're all the way he is. He understands them, speaks their language.

He even tells us places in the area we shouldn't go, where not to hang out because of the "elements" who are hanging around. Gambling, stuff like that. There are a couple of places that have already been closed down, not necessarily because the Giants blew the whistle or provided information, just because there was enough going on so that the police got interested. It's helpful to players who don't know the area, who don't know what goes on where, and that's another thing Bill tries to do to help the players, to keep them out of trouble. But some of the Giants used to visit these places, and that's when Bill got upset. As he always does, he called a few people, made a few contacts, found out about which ones were for real and which ones were sleazy, and then told us where he wouldn't like us to spend any time.

Another nice thing about Bill is that he tries to say something, even a little thing, to every player every day during the season, when we're in the locker room, on the field, just to make sure nobody thinks he's ignoring them. But generally, he leaves us alone in the locker room before the game, because it's a tight time for us. Sometimes I don't sleep the night before a game, especially if I'm going to be playing a good guy. Usually, what I want to do is establish myself in his mind sometime between the first and the fourth play of the game. I want him to know that I'm gonna be coming each play, all day long.

Guys get real tight and tense, sometimes they can't talk. The craziest guy around is L. T. I mean, he walks into the locker room thirty minutes before we're supposed to be dressed and on the field, and he's yelling and giving everybody shit and he's always the last one to get dressed, him and Byron Hunt. You see different players get ready in different ways. The closest I ever saw a player come to missing a game was Bobby Johnson before the championship game last year. That was wild, man. We were about to go out on the field and he walks in at noon. He never said where he was. I'm sure he got fined. You're supposed to be there two hours before the game; some guys show up at nine in the morning, guys like Benson and Martin.

But every team is different, every player on a team needs a different way of getting ready, and Bill realizes this and leaves us to ourselves before a game.

I don't see any players taking any uppers, pills, stuff to get "more ready," you might say. There may be some guys on this team using steroids, but I don't know for sure. The most I ever saw in a locker room was when I was a rookie. Practice was over, and there was a former player, smoking a cigarette. That was the wildest shit I'd ever seen, I never expected to see a pro player smoking, and I said to myself, hey, son, welcome to the NFL. I don't think any of the players even smoke these days, and that's good because we have an image to protect. There used to be some minor problem with drugs but no more. Parcells took care of that, too.

Now he's got intelligent players with level heads, and when you have those kinds of players, you don't have much of a drug problem or any other kind of problem. That kind of athlete realizes that everything you do becomes part of your resume. You don't have any trouble with guys who want to make something happen for themselves after football, who want to get established in an area, be involved in the community, in some kind of business.

Bill understands us. He's a player's coach, and there are times when I think he lets us get away with stuff. I've been able to sneak out of training camp two or three times to see Annette; I had her staying in the Ramada Inn up near Pleasantville, and sometimes I stay all night. But I think Bill is aware of stuff like that, because if he wasn't, We wouldn't be getting away with anything.

He can be very strict. He knows when it's okay to be a little loose, but most of the time he's right on the line. I remember when we were in Dallas two years ago, we had a player named Frank Cephous. He snuck out the night before a game and got caught. That's a $1,000 fine and I don't think Frank was making that much money to be able to really afford it. So he's trying to tell Bill it was his mother he went to see, and she was staying in the hotel just across the street. But then Bill says he knows it wasn't his mother, and this, that and the other thing; the man didn't care about whether it was his mother or not. The

fact that he left the hotel and wasn't supposed to was all
that counted. So he banged him for a thousand bucks,
and I just hope she was worth it, because that's a lot of
money to be paying for a couple of hours.

We have a few $1,000 fines like that. Not showing up
for a practice is one. Breaking curfew is $500, I believe.
Staying out all night is a $1,000, so is losing your play-
book. It's even a hundred bucks if you're caught eating in
a meeting, and I don't really agree with that. It's not bad if
you were allowed to bring in a piece of fruit or something,
but that's a hundred bucks if they really want to put it to
you, you know?

I mean, at that kind of meeting it's sometimes so
boring guys fall asleep. That's something Bill doesn't seem
anxious to change. We can watch forty minutes of film at
a time, and I think it should never be any more than
twenty minutes, and then break for five minutes and
come back and do some more. That's the deal. But forty
minutes of talking and pulling out papers and going through
the game plan—you just don't get anything accomplished.
A player isn't gonna remember stuff like that. I've said
that, but Bill hasn't changed anything.

Hey, he's the coach. And we did win the Super Bowl.
And he's my friend, too. So whatever he says is what I'll
do. Almost all the time. It's not the end of the line for me.

1986 GIANTS ROSTER

HEAD COACH: Bill Parcells

ASSISTANT COACHES: Bill Belichick, Linebackers; Romeo Crennel, Special Teams; Ron Erhardt, Offensive Coordinator; Len Fontes, Defensive Backfield; Ray Hanley, Running Backs; Fred Hoaglin, Offensive Line; Pat Hodgson, Receivers; Lamar Leachman, Defensive Line; Johnny Parker, Strength and Conditioning; Mike Pope, Tight Ends; Mike Sweatman, Assistant Special Teams.

NO.	NAME	POS.	HT.	WT.	YRS.	AGE	COLLEGE
2	Allegre, Raul	K	5-10	161	3	27	University of Texas
24	Anderson, Ottis	RB	6-2	225	8	29	Miami
67	Ard, Bill	G	6-3	270	6	27	Wake Forest
58	Banks, Carl	LB	6-4	235	3	24	Michigan State
89	Bavaro, Mark	TE	6-4	245	2	23	Notre Dame
60	Benson, Brad	T	6-3	270	9	31	Penn State
64	Burt, Jim	NT	6-1	260	6	27	Miami
53	Carson, Harry	LB	6-2	240	11	33	South Carolina State
44	Carthon, Maurice	RB	6-1	225	2	25	Arkansas State
25	Collins, Mark	CB	5-10	190	R	22	Cal St. Fullerton
77	Dorsey, Eric	DE	6-5	280	R	22	Notre Dame
28	Flynn, Tom	S	6-0	195	3	24	Pittsburgh
30	Galbreath, Tony	RB	6-0	228	11	32	Missouri
61	Godfrey, Chris	G	6-3	265	4	28	Michigan
54	Headen, Andy	LB	6-5	242	4	26	Clemson
48	Hill, Kenny	S	6-0	195	6	28	Yale
74	Howard, Eric	NT	6-4	268	R	22	Washington State
57	Hunt, Bryon	LB	6-5	242	6	28	SMU
88	Johnson, Bob	WR	5-11	171	3	25	Kansas
68	Johnson, Damian	T	6-5	290	1	24	Kansas State
52	Johnson, Thomas	LB	6-3	248	R	22	Ohio State
59	Johnston, Brian	C	6-3	275	1	24	North Carolina
51	Jones, Robbie	LB	6-2	230	3	27	Alabama
5	Landeta, Sean	P	6-0	200	2	24	Towson State
46	Lasker, Greg	S	6-0	200	R	22	Arkansas
70	**Marshall, Leonard**	**DE**	**6-3**	**285**	**4**	**25**	**LSU**
75	Martin, George	DE	6-4	255	12	33	Oregon
80	McConkey, Phil	WR	5-10	170	3	29	Navy
87	Miller, Solomon	WR	6-1	185	R	22	Utah State
20	Morris, Joe	RB	5-7	195	5	26	Syracuse
84	Mowatt, Zeke	TE	6-3	240	3	25	Florida State
63	Nelson, Karl	T	6-6	285	3	26	Iowa State
65	Oates, Bart	C	6-3	265	2	28	Brigham Young
34	Patterson, Elvis	CB	5-11	188	3	26	Kansas

NO.	NAME	POS.	HT.	WT.	YRS.	AGE	COLLEGE
55	Reasons, Gary............LB		6-4	234	3	24	NW Louisiana State
66	Roberts, William...........T		6-5	280	2	24	Ohio State
81	Robinson, Stacy.........,.WR		5-11	186	2	24	North Dakota State
22	Rouson, Lee..............RB		6-1	210	2	24	Colorado
17	Rutledge, Jeff.............QB		6-1	195	8	29	Alabama
78	Sally, Jerome.............NT		6-3	270	5	27	Missouri
11	Simms, Phil..............QB		6-3	214	8	30	Morehead State
56	Taylor, Lawrence..........LB		6-3	243	6	27	North Carolina
73	Washington, John..........DE		6-4	275	R	23	Oklahoma State
27	Welch, Herb..............DB		5-11	180	2	25	UCLA
23	Williams, Perry............CB		6-2	203	3	25	North Carolina State

GIANTS STATISTICS—
1986 REGULAR SEASON

WON 14, LOST 2

September	8	L	28-31	at Dallas	59,804
September	14	W	20-7	San Diego	74,921
September	21	W	14-9	at Raiders	71,164
September	28	W	20-17	New Orleans	72,769
October	5	W	13-6	at St. Louis	40,562
October	12	W	35-3	Philadelphia	74,221
October	19	L	12-17	at Seattle	62,282
October	27	W	27-20	Washington	75,923
November	2	W	17-14	Dallas	74,871
November	9	W	17-14	at Philadelphia	60,601
November	16	W	22-20	at Minnesota	62,003
November	23	W	19-16	Denver	75,116
December	1	W	21-17	at San Francisco	59,777
December	7	W	24-14	at Washington	55,642
December	14	W	27-7	St. Louis	75,261
December	20	W	55-24	Green Bay	71,351

TEAM STATISTICS

	Giants	Opp.			
TOTAL FIRST DOWNS	324	284	**NET YARDS PASSING**	3133	3473
Rushing	127	78	Avg. Per Game	195.8	217.1
Passing	171	177	Tackled/Yards Lost	46/367	59/414
Penalty	26	29	Gross Yards	3500	3887
3rd Down: Made/Att	85/228	75/212	Att./Completions	472/260	587/334
4th Down: Made/Att	10/ 14	2/ 11	Completion Pct.	55.1	56.9
			Had Intercepted	22	24
TOTAL NET YARDS	5378	4757	**PUNTS/AVERAGE**	79/ 44.8	89/ 39.3
Avg. Per Game	336.1	297.3			
Total Plays	1076	996	**NET PUNTING AVG.**	37.1	34.5
Avg. Per Play	5.0	4.8	**PENALTIES/YARDS**	96/738	120/988
NET YARDS RUSHING	2245	1284	**FUMBLES/BALL LOST**	31/10	36/19
Avg. Per Game	140.3	80.3			
Total Rushes	558	350	**TOUCHDOWNS**	42	26
			Rushing	18	10
			Passing	22	15
			Returns	2	1

INDIVIDUAL STATISTICS

PASSING	Att	Comp	Yds	Pct	Yds/Att	TD	Int	LG	Rating
Simms	468	259	3487	55.3	7.45	21	22	49	74.6
Rutledge	3	1	13	33.3	4.33	1	0	t13	87.5
Galbreath	1	0	0	0.0	0.00	0	0	0	39.6
GIANTS	472	260	3500	55.1	7.42	22	22	49	75.0
OPPONENTS	587	334	3887	56.9	6.62	15	24	t75	68.6

RUSHING	NO	YDS	AVG	LG	TD
Morris	341	1516	4.4	54	14
Carthon	72	260	3.6	12	0
Anderson, StL-Gts	75	237	3.2	16	3
Anderson, Gts	24	81	3.4	16	1
Rouson	54	179	3.3	t21	2
Simms	43	72	1.7	18	1
Galbreath	16	61	3.8	10	0
B. Johnson	2	28	14.0	22	0
Manuel	1	25	25.0	25	0
Rutledge	3	19	6.3	18	0
Miller	1	3	3.0	3	0
Hostetler	1	1	1.0	1	0
GIANTS	558	2245	4.0	54	18
OPPONENTS	350	1284	3.7	50	10

RECEIVING	NO	YDS	AVG	LG	TD
Bavaro	66	1001	15.2	41	4
Galbreath	33	268	8.1	19	0
B. Johnson	31	534	17.2	t44	5
Robinson	29	494	17.0	49	2
Morris	21	233	11.1	23	1
Anderson, StL-Gts	19	137	7.2	19	0
Anderson, Gts	9	46	5.1	12	0
McConkey	16	279	17.4	46	1
Carthon	16	67	4.2	10	0
Manuel	11	181	16.5	35	3
Mowatt	10	119	11.9	30	2
Miller	9	144	16.0	t32	2
Rouson	8	121	15.1	t37	1
Carson	1	13	13.0	t13	1
GIANTS	260	3500	13.5	49	22
OPPONENTS	334	3887	11.6	t75	15

SCORING	TDR	TDP	TDRt	PAT	FG	S	TP
Allegre	0	0	0	33/33	24/32	0	105
Morris	14	1	0	0/0	0/0	0	90
B. Johnson	0	5	0	0/0	0/0	0	30
Bavaro	0	4	0	0/0	0/0	0	24
Anderson, StL-Gts	3	0	0	0/0	0/0	0	18
Anderson, Gts	1	0	0	0/0	0/0	0	6
Manuel	0	3	0	0/0	0/0	0	18
Rouson	2	1	0	0/0	0/0	0	18
Miller	0	2	0	0/0	0/0	0	12
Mowatt	0	2	0	0/0	0/0	0	12
Robinson	0	2	0	0/0	0/0	0	12
Cooper	0	0	0	4/4	2/4	0	10
Carson	0	1	0	0/0	0/0	0	6
Flynn	0	0	1	0/0	0/0	0	6
Martin	0	0	1	0/0	0/0	0	6
McConkey	0	1	0	0/0	0/0	0	6
Simms	1	0	0	0/0	0/0	0	6
Thomas	0	0	0	4/4	0/1	0	4
GIANTS	18	22	2	41/42	26/37	0	371
OPPONENTS	10	15	1	26/26	18/25	0	236

FIELD GOALS	1-19	20-29	30-39	40-49	50+
Allegre	0/0	10/11	8/8	6/11	0/2
Cooper	0/0	2/2	0/1	0/0	0/0
Thomas	0/0	0/0	0/1	0/0	0/0
GIANTS	0/0	12/13	8/10	6/12	0/2
OPPONENTS	0/0	6/6	8/11	4/7	0/1

INTERCEPTIONS	NO	YDS	AVG	LG	TD
Kinard	4	52	13.0	25	0
Williams	4	31	7.8	15	0
Hill	3	25	8.3	23	0
Reasons	2	28	14.0	18	0
Patterson	2	26	13.0	26	0
Welch	2	22	11.0	16	0
Martin	1	78	78.0	t78	1
Carson	1	20	20.0	20	0
P. Johnson	1	13	13.0	13	0
Headen	1	1	1.0	1	0
Collins	1	0	0.0	0	0
Flynn, G.B.-Gts	1	0	0.0	0	0
Lasker	1	0	0.0	0	0
Marshall	**1**	**0**	**0.0**	**0**	**0**
GIANTS	24	296	12.3	t78	1
OPPONENTS	22	218	9.9	t58	1

PUNTING	NO	YDS	AVG	TB	In20	LG	BK
Landeta	79	3539	44.8	11	24	61	0
GIANTS	79	3539	44.8	11	24	61	0
OPPONENTS	89	3499	39.3	7	15	59	1

PUNT RETURNS	RET	FC	YDS	AVG	LG	TD
McConkey	32	12	253	7.9	22	0
Collins	3	1	11	3.7	6	0
Galbreath	3	1	1	0.3	1	0
Manuel	3	6	22	7.3	12	0
GIANTS	41	20	287	7.0	22	0
OPPONENTS	41	14	386	9.4	61	0

KICKOFF RETURNS	NO	YDS	AVG	LG	TD
McConkey	24	471	19.6	27	0
Collins	11	204	18.5	26	0
Miller	7	111	15.9	23	0
Hill	5	61	12.2	30	0
Rouson	2	21	10.5	12	0
Lasker	1	0	0.0	0	0
GIANTS	50	868	17.4	30	0
OPPONENTS	70	1362	19.5	57	0

SCORING	1	2	3	4	OT	TOTAL
GIANTS	40	130	106	95	0	371
OPPONENTS	39	84	37	76	0	236

1986 PLAYOFFS—
ALL GAMES COMBINED

WON 3, LOST 0

January 4	W	49- 3	San Francisco	76,034
January 11	W	17- 0	Washington	76,633
January 25	W	39-20	Denver	101,063

TEAM STATISTICS

	Giants	Opponents
TOTAL FIRST DOWNS	57	44
Rushing	30	9
Passing	22	29
Penalty	5	6
3rd Down: Made/Att	15/39	9/42
4th Down: Made/Att	3/5	0/4
TOTAL NET YARDS	964	746
Avg. Per Game	321.3	248.7
Total Plays	190	192
Avg. Per Play	5.1	3.9
NET YARDS RUSHING	469	121
Avg. Per Game	156.3	40.3
Total Rushes	128	55
NET YARDS PASSING	495	625
Avg. Per Game	165.0	208.3
Tackled/Yards Lost	3/22	9/84
Gross Yards	517	709
Att./Completions	59/39	128/61
Completion Pct.	66.1	47.7
Had Intercepted	0	5
PUNTS/AVERAGE	16/43.7	21/38.2
NET PUNTING AVG.	38.8	33.0
PENALTIES/YARDS	15/119	18/105
FUMBLES/BALL LOST	4/3	7/2
TOUCHDOWNS	14	2
Rushing	5	1
Passing	8	1
Returns	1	0

INDIVIDUAL STATISTICS

PASSING	Att.	Comp.	Yards	Pct.	Avg./ Att.	TD	Int.	LG	Rating
Simms	58	38	494	65.5	8.52	8	0	44	131.8
Rutledge	1	1	23	100.0	23.00	0	0	23	118.8
GIANTS	59	39	517	66.1	8.76	8	0	44	133.3
OPPONENTS	128	61	709	47.7	5.54	1	5	54	51.2

RUSHING	No.	Yds.	Avg.	LG	TD
Morris	73	313	4.4	t45	4
Rouson	12	52	4.3	18	0
Carthon	16	49	3.1	10	0
Simms	11	38	3.5	22	0
Galbreath	5	16	3.2	7	0
Anderson	7	6	0.9	3	1
Rutledge	3	0	0.0	2	0
Manuel	1	-5	-5.0	-5	0
GIANTS	128	469	3.7	t45	5
OPPONENTS	55	121	2.2	12	1

RECEIVING	No.	Yds.	Avg.	LG	TD
Bavaro	8	134	16.8	30	2
Carthon	8	38	4.8	8	0
Manuel	5	79	15.8	25	1
Morris	5	22	4.4	12	0
McConkey	3	78	26.0	44	2
Robinson	3	62	20.7	36	0
Rouson	3	45	15.0	23	0
Mowatt	2	35	17.5	t29	2
B. Johnson	1	15	15.0	t15	1
Galbreath	1	9	9.0	9	0
GIANTS	39	517	13.3	44	8
OPPONENTS	61	709	11.6	54	1

INTERCEPTIONS	No.	Yds.	Avg.	LG	TD
Taylor	1	34	34.0	t34	1
P. Johnson	1	27	27.0	27	0
Reasons	1	15	15.0	15	0
Patterson	1	9	9.0	16	0
Welch	1	0	0.0	0	0
GIANTS	5	85	17.0	t34	1

SCORING	TDR	TDP	TDRt	PAT	FG	S	TP
Morris	4	0	0	0/ 0	0/0	0	24
Allegre	0	0	0	13/14	2/2	0	19
Bavaro	0	2	0	0/ 0	0/0	0	12
McConkey	0	2	0	0/ 0	0/0	0	12
Mowatt	0	2	0	0/ 0	0/0	0	12
Anderson	1	0	0	0/ 0	0/0	0	6
B. Johnson	0	1	0	0/ 0	0/0	0	6
Manuel	0	1	0	0/ 0	0/0	0	6
Taylor	0	0	1	0/ 0	0/0	0	6
Martin	0	0	0	0/ 0	0/0	1	2
GIANTS	5	8	1	13/14	2/2	1	105
OPPONENTS	1	1	0	2/ 2	3/5	0	23

PUNTING	No.	Yds.	Avg.	TB	In20	LG	TD
Landeta	16	699	43.7	2	3	59	0
GIANTS	16	699	43.7	2	3	59	0
OPPONENTS	21	802	38.2	0	4	49	0

PUNT RETURNS	Ret	FC	Yds.	Avg.	LG	TD
McConkey	13	2	109	8.4	25	0
GIANTS	13	2	109	8.4	25	0
OPPONENTS	6	4	39	6.5	10	0

KICKOFF RETURNS	No.	Yds.	Avg.	LG	TD
Rouson	4	73	18.3	22	0
Flynn	1	-3	-3.0	-3	0
Hill	1	15	15.0	15	0
GIANTS	6	85	14.2	22	0
OPPONENTS	14	218	15.6	29	0

FIELD GOALS	1-19	20-29	30-39	40-49	50 +
Allegre	0/0	1/1	0/0	1/1	0/0
OPPONENTS	0/0	2/3	0/1	1/1	0/0

SCORE BY PERIODS

	1	2	3	4	OT	Total
GIANTS	24	30	38	13	0	105
OPPONENTS	13	0	0	10	0	23

DEFENSIVE STATISTICS—
1986 REGULAR SEASON

TACKLES	(G-GS)*	Solos	Assists	Total
Carl Banks	(16-16)	87	33	120
Harry Carson	(16-16)	87	31	118
Lawrence Taylor	(16-16)	79	26	105
Gary Reasons	(16-16)	57	39	96
Kenny Hill	(16-16)	45	23	68
Jim Burt	(13-13)	40	21	61
Leonard Marshall	**(16-16)**	**38**	**22**	**60**
Mark Collins	(15- 9)	45	15	60
Terry Kinard	(14-14)	42	17	59
Perry Williams	(16-16)	49	8	57
Elvis Patterson	(13- 7)	43	10	53
George Martin	(16-16)	32	17	49
Andy Headen	(16- 0)	26	14	40
Pepper Johnson	(16- 0)	26	11	37
Herb Welch	(16- 2)	29	8	37
Jerome Sally	(16- 2)	17	11	28
Greg Lasker	(16- 0)	22	6	28
Byron Hunt	(16- 0)	14	9	23
Robbie Jones	(16- 0)	13	3	16
Erik Howard	(9- 2)	9	5	14
Lee Rouson	(14- 1)	12	1	13
Bobby Johnson	(16-15)	6	0	6
Solomon Miller	(16- 4)	6	0	6
Eric Dorsey	(16- 0)	2	3	5
Zeke Mowatt	(16- 1)	3	1	4
Stacy Robinson	(12-10)	2	0	2
John Washington	(16- 0)	2	0	2
Bart Oates	(16-16)	2	0	2
Tony Galbreath	(16- 0)	2	0	2
Billy Ard	(16-16)	2	0	2
Brad Benson	(16-16)	1	0	1
Karl Nelson	(16-16)	1	0	1
Phil Simms	(16-16)	1	0	1
Chris Godfrey	(16-16)	1	0	1
Maurice Carthon	(16-16)	1	0	1
Tom Flynn	(2- 0)	0	1	1

*Games—Games Started

QUARTERBACK SACKS 59

Lawrence Taylor 20½-137
Leonard Marshall 12-86½
Carl Banks 6½-52½
Jerome Sally 3½-25
George Martin 3-21
Andy Headen 2½-23
Pepper Johnson 2-16
Erik Howard 2-12
Harry Carson 2-15
Terry Kinard 1-9
Jim Burt 1-9
Kenny Hill 1-9
Perry Williams 1-6
Greg Lasker 1-2

FUMBLE RECOVERIES 19

Leonard Marshall (3); Jim Burt (3); Carl Banks (2); Harry Carson (2); Terry Kinard (2); Kenny Hill (2); Mark Collins (1); Mark Bavaro (1); George Martin (1); Zeke Mowatt (1); Herb Welch (1)

FORCED FUMBLES 23

Leonard Marshall (3); Lawrence Taylor (3); George Martin (2); Carl Banks (2); Greg Lasker (2); Kenny Hill (2); Harry Carson (2); Terry Kinard (1); Andy Headen (1); Mark Collins (1); Bobby Johnson (1); Perry Williams (1); Gary Reasons (1); Jim Burt (1)

BLOCKED KICKS 2

Tom Flynn (blocked punt and 36-yard TD return vs. Green Bay, 12/20); Jeff Hostetler (partially blocked punt vs. Philadelphia, 11/9)

1986 POST-SEASON
INDIVIDUAL HONORS

BILL PARCELLS: NFL Coach of the Year (PFWA, AP, UPI, Sporting News, Football News, Pro Football Weekly, Football Digest, College & Pro Football Newsweekly)

LAWRENCE TAYLOR: Pro Bowl
NFL Most Valuable Player (PFWA, AP, Sporting News, Football Digest)
Defensive Most Valuable Player (AP, NEA, Pro Football Weekly)
All-NFL (AP, NEA, PFWA, UPI, Sporting News, Football News, Sports Illustrated)

PHIL SIMMS: Super Bowl MVP
All-NFL (NEA)
NFL Most Valuable Player (NEA)
All-NFC (Football News)
Pro Bowl Alternate

JOE MORRIS: Pro Bowl
NFL Player of the Year (Football News)
All-NFL (AP, PFWA, NEA, UPI, Sporting News, Pro Football Weekly)

MARK BAVARO: Pro Bowl
All-NFL (AP, PFWA, UPI, Sporting News, Pro Football Weekly)

SEAN LANDETA: Pro Bowl
All-NFL (AP, PFWA, UPI, Sporting News, Pro Football Weekly)

JIM BURT: Pro Bowl
All-NFL (Pro Football Weekly)

HARRY CARSON: Pro Bowl
All-NFC (Pro Football Weekly, Football News, UPI)
2d team All-NFL (AP, NEA)

LEONARD MARSHALL: **Pro Bowl**
2d team All-NFL (AP)
2d team All-NFC (UPI)

BRAD BENSON: Pro Bowl
2d team All-NFL (AP)

CARL BANKS: Pro Bowl alternate
Honorable Mention All-NFL (AP)

CHRIS GODFREY: 2d Team All-NFC (UPI)
                    Honorable Mention All-NFL (AP)

BILLY ARD: Pro Bowl alternate
                    Honorable Mention All-NFL (AP)

BART OATES: Pro Bowl alternate
                    Honorable Mention All-NFL (AP)

MARK COLLINS: All-NFL Rookie team (Pro Football Weekly)

RAUL ALLEGRE: Honorable Mention All-NFL (AP)

1986 RECORD BOOK PERFORMANCES

TEAM RECORDS SET IN 1986

Most victories, regular season	14
Most consecutive victories	9[1]
Most victories at home, season	8
Most points scored first period, game (vs. Green Bay 12/20)	21
Most field goals attempted, game (vs. Minnesota 11/16)	6[2]

INDIVIDUAL RECORDS SET IN 1986

Joe Morris, Most yards rushing, season	1,516
Joe Morris, Most rushing attempts, season	341
Joe Morris, Most games, 100 yards rushing, career	16
Joe Morris, Most games, 100 yards rushing, season	8
Joe Morris, Highest rushing average, career (818-3,555)	4.35
Joe Morris, Most rushing touchdowns, career	40
Joe Morris, Most rushing touchdowns, game	3*
Phil Simms, Most 300-yard passing games, career	15
Phil Simms, Most 300-yard passing games, season	4*
Mark Bavaro, Most receptions, tight end, season	66
Mark Bavaro, Most receiving yards, tight end, season	1,001
Lawrence Taylor, Most quarterback sacks, season	20½
Raul Allegre, Most field goals attempted, game	6*
Sean Landeta, Highest punting average, career (160-7011)	43.6*
Harry Carson, Most opponent fumbles recovered, game	2*
George Martin, Most defensive TDs, lineman, career (NFL record)	6

ATTENDANCE RECORDS SET IN 1986

Largest home attendance, season (turnstile count)	594,433
Largest road attendance, season (turnstile count)	471,835
Largest single game attendance, vs. Washington, Jan. 11, 1987	76,663

[1]Ties. (1962, 1927)
[2]Ties (four others)
*Tie

HOW THE GIANTS WERE BUILT

	DRAFT	TRADE	FREE AGENT
1975			
DE	George Martin (#11)		
1976			
LB	Harry Carson (#4)		
1977			
			G Brad Benson
1979			
QB	Phil Simms (#1)		
1980			
			DE Curtis McGriff, IR
1981			
LB	Lawrence Taylor (#1)		DT Jim Burt
G	Billy Ard (#8C)		
LB	Byron Hunt (#9)		
1982			
RB	Joe Morris (#2)	QB Jeff Rutledge (From L.A.)	NT Jerome Sally
1983			
S	Terry Kinard (#1), IR		TE Zeke Mowatt
DE	**Leonard Marshall (#2)**		
LB	Andy Headon (#8)		
T	Karl Nelson (#3)		
1984			
LB	Robbie Jones (#12)		
LB	Carl Banks (#1)	S Kenny Hill (From Raiders)	G Chris Godfrey
T	William Roberts (#1A)		
QB	Jeff Hostetler (#3), IR	RB Tony Galbreath (From Minn.)	WR Bobby Johnson
LB	Gary Reasons (#4A)		WR Phil McConkey
WR	Lionel Manuel (#7)		CB Elvis Patterson
G	David Jordan (#10), IR		

1985

RB	George Adams (#1), IR		RB	Maurice Carthon
WR	Stacy Robinson (#2)		P	Sean Landeta
CB	Tyrone Davis (#3), IR		C	Bart Oates
C	Brian Johnston (#3A)			
TE	Mark Bavaro (#4)			
RB	Lee Rouson (#8)			
S	Herb Welch (#12)			

1986

DE	Eric Dorsey (#1)	RB	Ottis Anderson	PK	Raul Allegre
CB	Mark Collins (#2)		(From St. Louis)	T	Damian Johnson
NT	Erik Howard (#2A)			S	Tom Flynn
LB	Pepper Johnson (#2B)				
S	Greg Lasker (#2C)				
DE	John Washington (#3), IR				
WR	Solomon Miller (#6A)				

ABOUT THE AUTHORS

LEONARD MARSHALL is the All Pro defensive end for the New York Giants. He was born and raised in Franklin, Louisiana, and now lives in New Jersey.

DAVE KLEIN is one of the deans of American sportswriting, with over 25 years' experience. Among his many books are *The Game of Their Lives, A Thinking Man's Guide to Pro Football*, and *Big Blue: A Giant Year*. He lives in New Jersey.